Trevor Baker, Adam Bayley, Andrew McAdam,
Matthew Priestley, Iain Wilson and Steve Wiseman

Exam Practice Workbook

OCR Twenty First Century
GCSE Physics A

Contents

Unit A181

- **3** Module P1: The Earth in the Universe
- **14** Module P2: Radiation and Life
- **24** Module P3: Sustainable Energy

Unit A182

- **35** Module P4: Explaining Motion
- **47** Module P5: Electric Circuits
- **59** Module P6: Radioactive Materials

Unit A183

- **70** Module P7: Further Physics – Studying the Universe

- **97** Data Sheet

- **1–12** Answers (found at the centre of the book)

The Earth in the Universe P1

1. (a) How long ago do scientists think the Earth was formed? Put a tick (✓) in the box next to the correct answer. [1]

3500 million years ago ☐

4500 million years ago ☐

4000 million years ago ☐

4500 years ago ☐

(b) Some people used to believe that the Earth was only 6000 years old. Suggest **two** reasons for this. [2]

1. ....

2. ....

2. (a) The diagram shows a wave. What is the wavelength of this wave? [1]

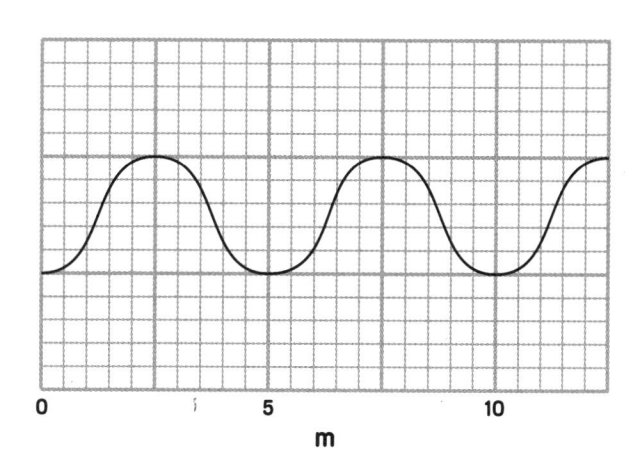

.... m

(b) Another wave has a wavelength of 10 metres and a speed of 4m/s. Calculate its frequency. [2]

.... Hz

© Lonsdale 3

P1 The Earth in the Universe

3. Alfred Wegener proposed the theory of continental drift.

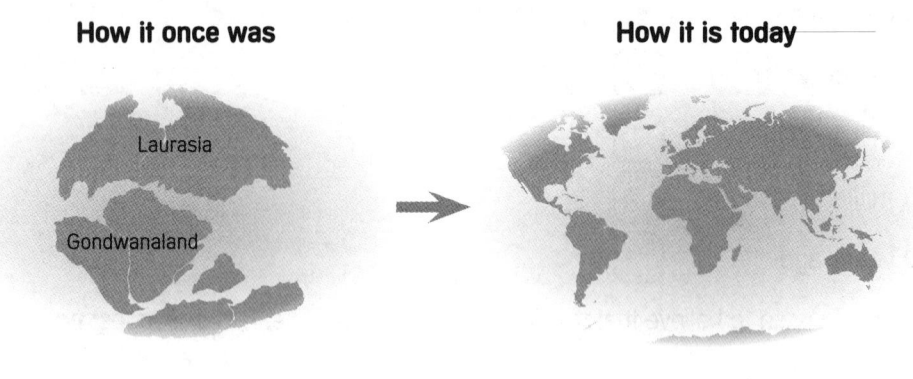

How it once was — Laurasia, Gondwanaland

How it is today

(a) Briefly outline the theory of continental drift. [2]

(b) Describe the evidence that Wegener put forward to support his theory and explain why many scientists did not accept this theory until further evidence was available.

The quality of written communication will be assessed in your answer to this question. [6]

The Earth in the Universe — P1

4. **(a)** What do scientists call the large pieces of rock that the Earth's crust is cracked into? Put a tick (✓) in the box next to the correct answer. [1]

Convection plates ☐

Conduction plates ☐

Tectonic plates ☐

Tectonic zones ☐

(b) What **three** major features can occur at plate boundaries? [3]

1. _____

2. _____

3. _____

(c) Complete the following description of how the seafloor spreads. Use words from this list. [4]

tectonic   liquid   constructive   magma   convection

Just below the crust the mantle is fairly solid. However, further down it is

_____ and able to move. _____ currents in the

mantle carry the _____ plates, moving entire continents. Where these

currents cause plates to move apart, _____ rises to the surface and new

areas of oceanic crust are formed.

5. State **three** ways in which tectonic plates can move at a plate boundary. [3]

1. _____

2. _____

3. _____

P1 The Earth in the Universe

6. **(a)** Of which type of plate boundary movement is California a good example? [1]

(b) Explain what happens at a constructive plate boundary and give an example. [3]

(c) Explain what happens at a destructive plate boundary and give an example. [3]

(d) What happens to an oceanic plate when it moves towards a continental plate? [2]

(e) Why do tectonic plates float on the Earth's mantle? Put a tick (✓) in the box next to the correct statement. [1]

Tectonic plates contain helium from meteorite strikes early in the Earth's past. ☐

Tectonic plates are less dense than the mantle and therefore float on top. ☐

Radioactive emissions from the Earth's core bombard the plates and cause them to float. ☐

Tectonic plates are stuck in position and therefore cannot sink. ☐

7. **(a)** Complete the following sentences. Use words from this list. [4]

fusion   gravity   heat   gas   friction

The solar system started as clouds of ………………………… and dust. These clouds were

pulled together by the force of …………………………, which created intense

…………………………. Nuclear ………………………… began and the Sun was formed.

The Earth in the Universe — P1

(b) Draw straight lines from the names of the different masses in the Universe to their correct description. [4]

Mass	Description
Asteroids	Small icy masses that orbit the Sun
Comets	Small rocky masses that orbit the Sun
Dwarf planets	Large masses that orbit the Sun
Moons	Large masses that have not cleared their orbits of other objects
Planets	Rocky masses that orbit planets

(c) Place the following planets in order of the length of time of their orbit. Put the letters in the empty boxes to show the correct order. Start with the shortest. [4]

A Mars **B** Mercury **C** Venus **D** Saturn **E** Jupiter

Shortest   Longest

8. (a) How old is our Sun? [1]

(b) Explain where the Sun's energy comes from. [2]

(c) Which of the following statements is true? Put a tick (✓) in the box next to the correct statement. [1]

- The Universe is approximately 5000 million years old. ☐
- The Sun is older than the Universe. ☐
- The Universe contains approximately a million galaxies. ☐
- The Earth is the same size as the Sun. ☐
- Our galaxy contains at least 100 billion stars. ☐

P1 The Earth in the Universe

(d) Place the following in order of size. Put the letters in the empty boxes to show the correct order. Start with the smallest. [4]

A The Universe B The Earth C The Sun
D The solar system E A galaxy

Smallest				Largest

(e) Explain what a light-year is and why scientists use them to measure distances in space. [2]

(f) The nearest galaxy to the Milky Way is 2.2 million light-years away. What does this mean about the light we observe from it today? [2]

(g) Name the **two** methods that astronomers can use to work out the distances to different stars. [2]

1.

2.

9. State **three** types of electromagnetic radiation given out by stars. [3]

1.

2.

3.

10. What is light pollution? [1]

The Earth in the Universe — P1

11. This question is about the origin of the Universe.

   (a) What is the 'Big Bang' theory? [1]

   (b) How many years ago do scientists think the 'Big Bang' happened? [1]

12. (a) Complete the following sentences. Use words from this list. You may use them more than once. [4]

   energy   light   matter   sound   travels   transfers

   All waves transfer .... from one place to another without transferring

   .... The .... is transferred in the direction the wave

   ....

   (b) (i) Describe the difference between longitudinal and transverse waves. [2]

   (ii) Give an example of each type of wave. [2]

   Longitudinal: ....

   Transverse: ....

   (c) (i) Explain what is meant by the **frequency** of a wave. [1]

   (ii) What is the unit for the frequency of a wave? [1]

P1 The Earth in the Universe

13. Harry and Robert are talking about where the Sun's energy comes from.

> **Harry**
> I think the Sun's energy comes from a chemical reaction. Just like when you burn a candle.

> **Robert**
> I think the Sun's energy comes from nuclear fusion. Hydrogen nuclei fuse to form heavier nuclei and some energy is released.

(a) Who is correct, Harry or Robert? [1]

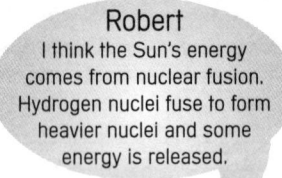

(b) The amount of energy released from the fusion between individual hydrogen nuclei is very small. How could this possibly explain the vast amounts of energy released? [2]

(c) Explain how the life cycle of a star can help to explain where all the elements come from.

✎ *The quality of written communication will be assessed in your answer to this question.* [6]

[Total: _____ / 86]

The Earth in the Universe — P1

Higher Tier

14. (a) Put a ring around the correct options in the following sentences. [2]

P-waves can travel through solids **and / but not** liquids.

S-waves can travel through solids **and / but not** liquids.

(b) Look at the diagram of a cross-section through the Earth.

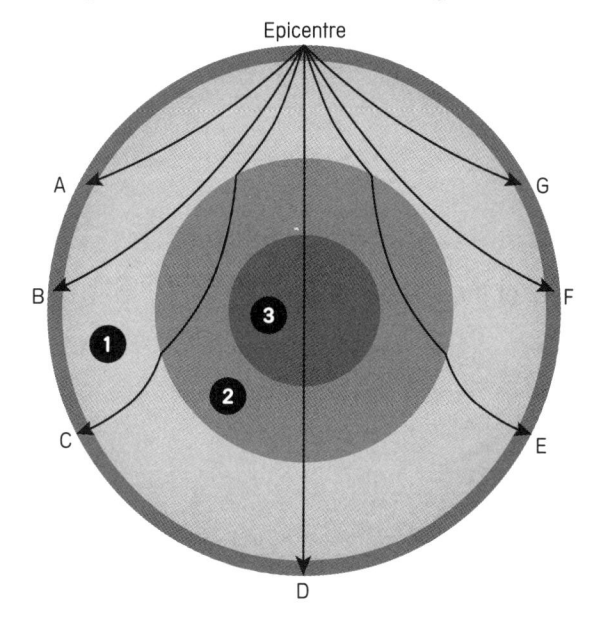

Key:
- ① = Mantle (solid)
- ② = Outer core (liquid)
- ③ = Inner core (solid)

(i) At which of the points, **A, B, C, D, E, F or G**, will P-waves be detected? [1]

(ii) At which of the points, **A, B, C, D, E, F or G**, will S-waves be detected? [1]

(c) Why do waves travel in curved paths through the Earth? [2]

(d) Why are there abrupt changes in the direction of the waves? [2]

P1 The Earth in the Universe

15. Explain how the pattern in the magnetisation of seafloor rocks on either side of oceanic ridges can provide evidence for tectonic theory.

✏ *The quality of written communication will be assessed in your answer to this question.* [6]

16. The diagram shows the movement of the tectonic plates.

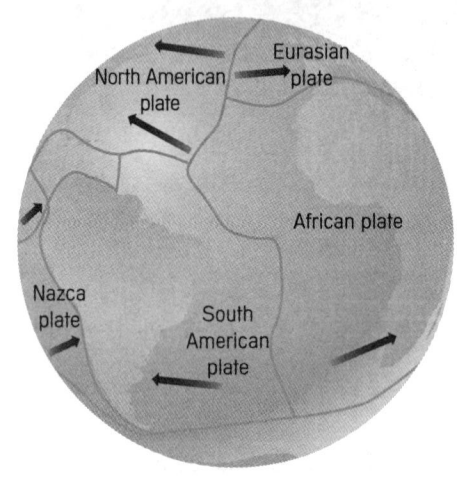

Describe how the movement of the tectonic plates is linked to the rock cycle. [6]

✏ *The quality of written communication will be assessed in your answer to this question.*

The Earth in the Universe — P1

17. Light from distant galaxies is red shifted. Use this information to explain why scientists think the Universe is expanding. [2]

18. (a) What does the future of the Universe depend on? [1]

(b) The Universe may end in a 'big crunch' or it may expand forever. State the conditions necessary for these two different possibilities to occur. [2]

'Big crunch': ....

Expand forever: ....

19. (a) Draw straight lines to join the seismic wave to its correct description. [1]

Seismic wave	Description
P-wave	Transverse
S-wave	Longitudinal

(b) The speed of seismic waves in the Earth's crust can be up to 8km/s but in the mantle the speed can be up to 13km/s. Explain why the speed is greater in the mantle. [3]

(c) An earthquake occurs at a depth of 40km within the Earth's crust. If the speed of the P-waves is 6km/s and the speed of the S-waves is 4km/s, calculate the time delay between the two waves reaching the surface. [3]

.... s

[Total: .... / 32]

P2 Radiation and Life

1. (a) What are the 'packets' of energy called that a beam of electromagnetic radiation carries? Put a tick (✓) in the box next to the correct answer. [1]

Protons ☐   Electrons ☐
Photons ☐   Neutrons ☐

(b) The electromagnetic spectrum can be arranged in order of wavelength. The regions **A, B, C** and **D** on the diagram are different parts of the electromagnetic spectrum. Write the correct letter in each box. [3]

A   B   C   D

Microwaves ☐   Infrared ☐
X-rays ☐   Gamma rays ☐

2. (a) Name **four** emitters of radiation and a detector that can be used for each one. [4]

Emitter 1: _____ Detector: _____

Emitter 2: _____ Detector: _____

Emitter 3: _____ Detector: _____

Emitter 4: _____ Detector: _____

(b) Materials can absorb, reflect or transmit radiation. Complete the sentences. Use words from this list. [2]

absorbed   **reflected**   **transmitted**

Microwaves are _____ when they hit a metal surface.

X-rays are _____ by bones.

Visible light is _____ by the atmosphere.

3. (a) Give **two** ways in which the intensity of electromagnetic radiation absorbed by an object can be reduced. [2]

_____

_____

_____

_____

Radiation and Life P2

(b) When photons are absorbed they can produce heat. What does the amount of heat produced depend on? [2]

....

....

4. A group of students is talking about exposure to the Sun.

Anna
My mother had skin cancer but she used to sunbathe a lot.

Tom
I stay indoors between 11am and 3pm when the Sun is at its hottest.

Grace
I go nice and brown in the sun.

Jack
I always use plenty of sun lotion and wear a T-shirt.

Emily
A little ultraviolet is good for you. It gives you vitamin D.

Kieran
I never burn in the sun and am unlikely to suffer any damage from ultraviolet rays.

(a) Which **two** students refer to actions taken to reduce the risks of exposure to ultraviolet radiation? [2]

.... and ....

(b) Which student refers to the dangers of ultraviolet radiation? .... [1]

(c) Which **two** students refer to the benefits of exposure to ultraviolet radiation? [2]

.... and ....

P2 Radiation and Life

5. Which of the statements about ionising radiation are correct? Put ticks (✓) in the boxes next to the **two** correct statements. [2]

Ionising radiation can break molecules into bits called ions. ☐

X-rays are a type of ionising radiation; gamma rays are not. ☐

Ionising radiation cannot break molecules into bits called ions. ☐

X-rays and gamma rays are types of ionising radiation. ☐

6. (a) Which of the following can be used to protect people from the effects of radiation? Put ticks (✓) in the boxes next to the **two** correct statements. [2]

Surrounding nuclear reactors with lead ☐

Wire screens in microwave ovens ☐

Staying in a swimming pool on a hot day ☐

Surrounding nuclear reactors with tin ☐

(b) Why is ionising radiation dangerous to humans? [2]

_____

_____

_____

(c) How do microwaves heat materials? [2]

_____

_____

7. (a) What effect will an increase in the amount of carbon dioxide in the atmosphere have on the Earth? Put a tick (✓) in the box next to the correct answer. [1]

The Earth will cool down. ☐

More radiation will escape. ☐

More heat will be absorbed by the atmosphere. ☐

There will be no effect. ☐

(b) Put a ring around the correct options in the following sentences. [3]

Light radiation from the Sun warms the Earth's surface and is used by plants for

respiration / photosynthesis. This process **increases / decreases** the amount of carbon dioxide

in the atmosphere and **increases / decreases** the amount of oxygen in the atmosphere.

Radiation and Life — P2

8. **(a)** Describe the effect that an increase in greenhouse gases has on the heat escaping into space. [1]

(b) Name the **three** main greenhouse gases. [3]

1.

2.

3.

9. How does the ozone layer help to protect us from radiation from the Sun?

✎ *The quality of written communication will be assessed in your answer to this question.* [6]

10. (a) The diagram shows the carbon cycle. Write the correct letter for each process in the boxes. [3]

Eating of plants ☐

Photosynthesis ☐

Respiration ☐

Death of plants and animals ☐

(b) Which process removes carbon dioxide from the atmosphere and which organisms take part in this process? [2]

P2 Radiation and Life

(c) Explain how the carbon from carbon dioxide in the atmosphere ends up in organisms further up the food chain and is then returned to the atmosphere.

The quality of written communication will be assessed in your answer to this question. [6]

(d) The amount of carbon dioxide in the atmosphere remained constant for thousands of years. Explain how. [2]

(e) Describe the two main processes which have contributed to the increase in carbon dioxide levels in recent times.

The quality of written communication will be assessed in your answer to this question. [6]

Radiation and Life — P2

11. **(a)** Although radio signals are not strongly absorbed by the atmosphere, they are not used to transmit signals to satellites. What properties of microwaves make them better suited for transmitting signals to satellites? Put ticks (✓) in the boxes next to the **two** correct statements. [2]

- They have higher energy. ☐
- They are significantly refracted by the atmosphere. ☐
- They have lower energy. ☐
- They are not significantly refracted by the atmosphere. ☐

(b) Name the type of radiation for each of the following uses. [4]

(i) Taking shadow pictures of bones: _____

(ii) Transmitting radio and TV programmes: _____

(iii) Satellite communication and heating food: _____

(iv) Carrying information along telephone cables: _____

(c) Explain how the properties of X-rays make them suitable for their use(s). [2]

_____

12. **(a)** A signal is often added to a high-energy carrier wave so that it can be transmitted long distances. This changes the carrier wave. This is called modulation. Which **two** features of a wave can be affected by modulation? Put ticks (✓) in the boxes next to the **two** correct answers. [2]

- Frequency ☐
- Type ☐
- Length ☐
- Amplitude ☐

(b) What is the role of a receiver in the transmission of information? [2]

_____

P2 Radiation and Life

13. **(a)** What is the main difference between an analogue signal and a digital signal? [1]

....

....

(b) Put a tick (✓) in the correct box to show whether each statement is **true** or **false**. [4]

	true	false
(i) Digital signals can take a range of values between 0 and 1.	☐	☐
(ii) The output of a digitally transmitted signal is of a higher quality than an analogue signal.	☐	☐
(iii) Noise can be easily removed so has little effect on digital signals.	☐	☐
(iv) Digital signals can only take two values: on or off.	☐	☐

(c) **(i)** On the grid provided, draw the digital signal represented by 1011001. [2]

(ii) On the grid provided, draw an analogue wave with a wavelength of 2cm and an amplitude of 1cm. [2]

(d) When talking about signals we often talk about 'noise'. What do we mean by signal noise? [1]

....

....

(e) Does the diagram show a received digital signal or a received analogue signal? [1]

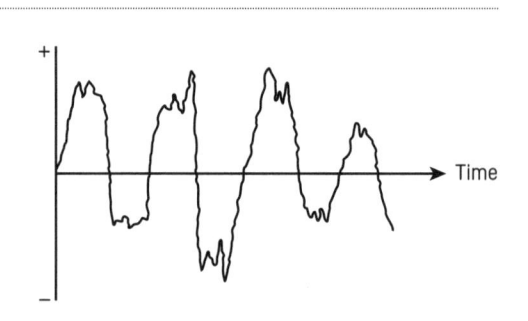

....

[Total: .... / 83]

Radiation and Life P2

Higher Tier

14. What **three** factors combine to cause a decrease in the intensity of electromagnetic radiation leaving the Sun's surface and reaching the Earth's atmosphere? [3]

1. _____
2. _____
3. _____

15. Complete the following sentence. [1]

The amount of damage to the skin caused by ultraviolet radiation depends on the intensity of the radiation and the _____ of exposure.

16 Put a ring around the correct options in the following sentence. [2]

Ions are **very reactive / unreactive** and **can / cannot** take part in further chemical reactions.

17. Sunbathing can put you at risk from ultraviolet radiation.

(a) State **two** ways in which you could reduce the risk of exposure to ultraviolet radiation. [2]

1. _____
2. _____

(b) What are the potential dangers of exposure to ultraviolet? [2]

_____
_____

P2 Radiation and Life

18. (a) Why do climatologists believe that human activity is responsible for global warming? [3]

(b) Use the carbon cycle to explain how burning forests affects the amount of carbon dioxide in the atmosphere.

✎ *The quality of written communication will be assessed in your answer to this question.* [6]

Radiation and Life P2

19. (a) The diagrams show an analogue signal and a digital signal which have been distorted by noise.

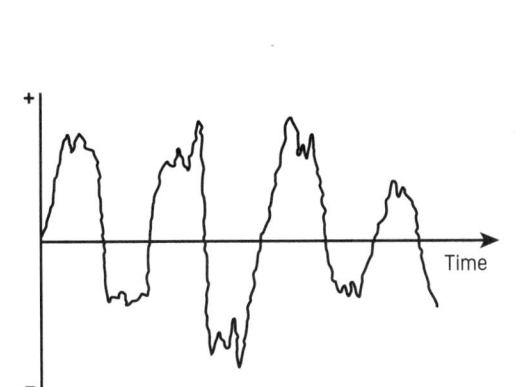

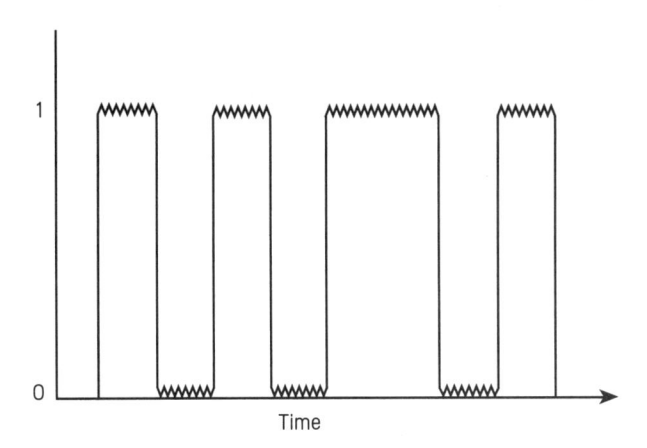

Explain why digital signals can be recovered after the addition of noise and why this is a benefit compared with analogue signals.

The quality of written communication will be assessed in your answer to this question. [6]

(b) Decide whether each statement applies to analogue signals, digital signals or both. [4]

(i) The signal is transmitted as an electromagnetic wave. ....

(ii) The signal is a code made up of 1s and 0s. ....

(iii) The signal is made up of short pulses. ....

(iv) The signal varies in the same way as the original sound wave. ....

[Total: .... / 29]

P3 Sustainable Energy

1. This question is about alternative power sources.

Charlie makes a model of a hydroelectric power station to show other students the advantages of alternative energy sources. In the model, water is static in a reservoir behind the dam. When water is allowed to flow from the reservoir, it causes a generator to produce electricity, which lights a 12V 36W lamp.

(a) Explain how the generator produces a voltage. [2]

A magnet revolves around inside a coil which produces a stream of electrons.

(b) (i) What energy changes take place in the model to enable the hydroelectric power station to produce electricity? [2]

(ii) When the generator is running, what is the value of the current flowing through the lamp? [2]

.... amps

(iii) If the lamp remains lit for 20 minutes, how much energy, in joules, will the lamp transfer? [2]

.... joules

(c) A group of students is talking about alternative energy sources.

Cindy: Using wave power might make the beach unsuitable for surfers.

Alex: I would rather use biofuel as it can be grown easily.

Hakeem: Hydroelectric power doesn't damage the atmosphere but it damages the environment in other ways.

Chloe: I don't think they should build a tidal power station. Trade would suffer.

(i) Which student is concerned about the effect one of the sources might have on tourism? [1]

Cindy

(ii) Which student is talking about a source that could produce greenhouse gases when burned? [1]

Alex

Sustainable Energy P3

2. This question is about primary and secondary energy sources.

(a) Which is **not** a primary energy source? Put a tick (✓) in the box next to the correct answer. [1]

Waves ☐   Heat ☐   Electrical ✓   Nuclear ☐   Wind ☐

(b) What do scientists mean when they describe an energy source as a **secondary energy source**? [1]

They man energy transferred from a primary to a secondary.

3. A new power station needs to be built near to the coast and the final decision will be either coal or nuclear as the primary energy source. The local environmental group is unhappy with both choices and feels that there are better solutions.

(a) Explain **one** problem with using coal and **one** problem with using nuclear power as the primary energy source. [2]

Coal: *Pollution to the Environment*

Nuclear power: *Hazardous waste,*

(b) Name **two** possible renewable energy sources and explain why the local environmental group might think that these alternative sources are an improvement.

🖉 *The quality of written communication will be assessed in your answer to this question.* [6]

P3 Sustainable Energy

4. The Sankey diagram gives information about the efficiency of energy transfers. Use the diagram to answer the questions below.

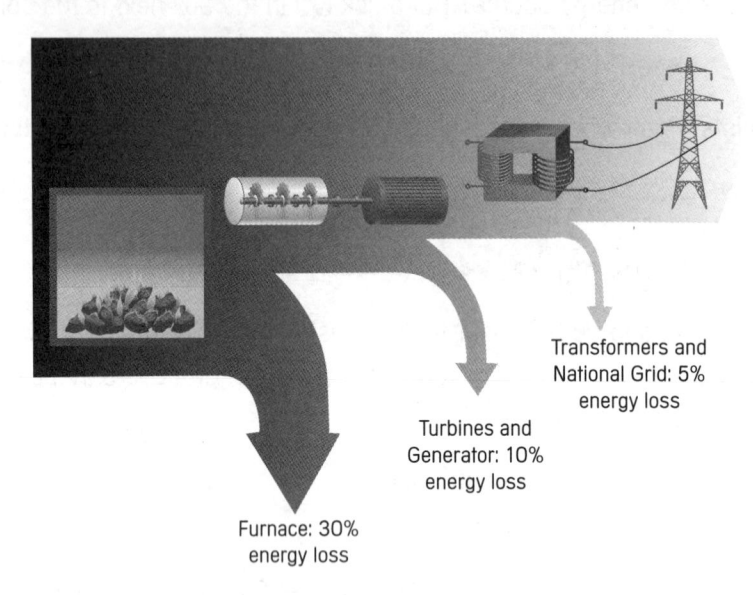

Transformers and National Grid: 5% energy loss

Turbines and Generator: 10% energy loss

Furnace: 30% energy loss

(a) What is the main form in which energy is lost during transfer? [1]

Heat

(b) How much energy is lost by transformers and the National Grid? [1]

5%

(c) What type of fuel could be put in the furnace? [1]

coal, wood

(d) For every 100J of energy stored in the coal, how much is reaching the mains supply in homes? Put a ring around the correct answer. [1]

10J   30J   40J   45J   **55J**

5. In a nuclear power station, uranium is used to produce electricity. Which statement correctly describes the process? Put a tick (✓) in the box next to the correct statement. [1]

Uranium is burned. Heat turns water into steam. Steam turns the generator. ☐

Fuel is burned. Heat turns water into steam. Steam turns a turbine. The turbine drives the generator. ☐

Energy is released from the nucleus. Heat is used to produce steam. Steam turns a turbine. The turbine drives the generator. ✓

Energy is released from the nucleus. Heat is used to turn water into steam. Steam turns the generator. ☐

Sustainable Energy — P3

6. A petrol generator produces an electric current by burning petrol, which is a primary fuel. Which statement below is correct about running a 12V 36W electric drill using the generator? Put a tick (✓) in the box next to the correct statement. [1]

Connecting a large resistance across the output terminals would increase the current to the drill. ☐

Running the generator for longer would increase the current to the drill. ☐

Drawing a larger current from the generator would use up more petrol each second. ☐

Changing the drill for one with a rating of 12V 24W would increase the current to the electric drill. ☐

7. Draw straight lines from each of the alternative energy sources to a question that has to be considered when using them. [2]

Alternative energy source	Question
Wind farm	Is there sufficient farmland available?
Biofuel	Is there a suitable place for a dam?
Hydroelectric power	Are there any hills to cause turbulence?

Lines drawn:
- Wind farm → Are there any hills to cause turbulence?
- Biofuel → Is there sufficient farmland available?
- Hydroelectric power → Is there a suitable place for a dam?

8. The table gives details on ways to save energy.

In the Home	In the Workplace	National Context
Use of more efficient appliances. A condensing boiler could save £190 per year	Cleaning air conditioner filters can save 5% of the energy used in running the system	Replace old houses with new efficient ones
Double glazing. Possible saving: £130 per year	Using low energy light bulbs	Increased use of public transport
Loft insulation. Possible saving: £145 per year	Roof insulation and cavity wall insulation in modern buildings	Use of more efficient trains and buses
Cavity wall insulation. Possible saving: £110 per year	Use of efficient, modern, low energy machinery	Encourage more widespread recycling
Draught proof rooms. Possible saving: £25 per year	Use of efficient, modern vehicles for transport of goods	Encourage car sharing and fewer journeys

You are a government minister for energy and have to advise on the best ways of saving energy in the home, in the workplace and in a national context.

P3 Sustainable Energy

(a) Name the **two** energy-saving measures in the home that save the most money. [2]

1. *Efficient devices*
2. *Double glazing.*

(b) How much money can be saved in the home over three years by adopting the two best energy-saving measures? [2]

£960 as £130 × 3 = 390 & £190 × 3 = 570
390 + 570 = £960

(c) Describe **one** way in which using low energy light bulbs can save money in the workplace. [1]

They can reduce the energy bill by using less energy for the same amount

(d) In the national context, how can more widespread recycling save energy?

✏️ The quality of written communication will be assessed in your answer to this question. [6]

9. The table shows changes to the energy sources used to generate electricity in the UK from 1990–2004.

Energy Source	% Used in 1990	% Used in 2004
Coal	67	33
Gas	0.05	40
Nuclear	18.9	19.2
Renewable sources	0	3.6
Hydroelectric power	1.1	2.6
Oil	6.8	1.1
Other	6.15	0.5

Sustainable Energy P3

The availability of cheap gas from the North Sea and concerns about pollution and the price of oil have had an effect on the energy sources used in the UK.

Which are **not** true explanations of the data in the table? Put ticks (✓) in the boxes next to the **two incorrect** statements. [2]

Supplies of coal from British mines ran out in the 1990s. ✓

The use of nuclear power remained roughly constant throughout the period. ☐

The use of gas in power stations increased substantially between 1990 and 2004. ☐

The use of hydroelectric power increased after 1990 due to increased rainfall. ✓

Renewable sources were not seriously considered as a main energy source in 1990. ☐

The use of oil in power stations fell due to the rise in price after 1990. ☐

10. This question is about using electricity to power items in the home.

The table gives some information about electrical items and how long they were used for.

Electrical Appliance	Power Rating	Time Used For
Electric heater	4kW	90 minutes
Lamp	100W	8 hours
Electric fire	3000W	30 minutes
Kettle	3000W	2 minutes

The cost of electricity is 8p per unit (kWh).

(a) How much would it cost for the lamp? [2]

(b) If the water inside the kettle receives 1800 joules of energy every second, how efficient is the kettle? [2]

P3 Sustainable Energy

11. Below is a chart showing the production of two primary fuels between 1980 and 2010 in the UK.

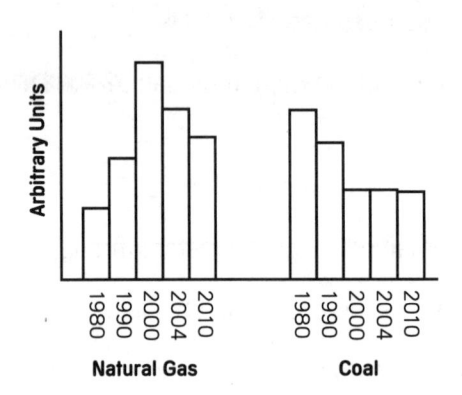

(a) (i) The mass of coal mined fell between 1980 and 2000 but gas production increased during the same period. Suggest why this might have happened. [1]

Less jobs for coal in demand for oil increase, coal ran out

(ii) An energy minister said: "No new coal power stations have been built in the UK for the last 10 years." How does the chart support this comment? [1]

(b) A student comments that there are limitations to the conclusions that can be made from the data. What is the main limitation that lowers confidence in any conclusion made? [1]

12. A farmer in Scotland is interested in using her land to generate electricity for the National Grid. She is keen on renewable sources and is unsure whether to choose biofuel, wind or solar as her source for generating electricity. She is advised to use wind turbines by a friend. What reasons might her friend have given for this choice?

The quality of written communication will be assessed in your answer to this question. [6]

Sustainable Energy — P3

13. Below are three boxes containing a type of renewable energy source and three boxes containing statements about alternative energy. Draw straight lines to join each source to the correct statement. [2]

Source	Statement
Solar	Build in exposed areas
Hydroelectric	A dam needs to be built across a river
Wind	It is ideal if the panels face south

(Solar → It is ideal if the panels face south; Hydroelectric → A dam needs to be built across a river; Wind → Build in exposed areas)

14. This question is about how the generation of energy from alternative sources could replace current power stations.

(a) The Government needs to build new power stations to meet the country's energy needs. The choice is between using fossil fuels or nuclear fuel to power them. Give **one** advantage and **one** disadvantage of using any one named fossil fuel and **one** advantage and **one** disadvantage of using nuclear fuel. [4]

One advantage of coal is that it requires less supervision. A disadvantage is pollution. One advantage of Nuclear is no pollution. One disadvantage is ...

(b) (i) People are concerned about building new power stations that burn fossil fuels. Some suggest that only wind farms should be built. Give **two** reasons why this is not a good idea. [2]

1. *Noise*

2. *Some days its not windy*

(ii) The Government believes that some of our energy requirements could be supplied from wind turbines. It prefers to build new wind farms out at sea. Give **two** advantages and **two** disadvantages of having the wind farms out at sea. [4]

Advantage 1: *No uncomfort to humans*

Advantage 2: *More spacious.*

Disadvantage 1: *Hard to maintain*

Disadvantage 2: *Danger to wildlife*

P3 Sustainable Energy

(iii) Wind turbines drive the turbine directly. Give **two** other examples of renewable sources that also drive turbines directly. [2]

1. ~~~~~~~~~~~~~~~~
2. ~~~~~~~~~~~~~~~~

[Total: .... / 68]

Higher Tier

15. The table gives information about some of the energy sources used in the United Kingdom.

Energy Source	Problems	Additional Information
Gas	Increase in gas imports as the North Sea supplies fall	Supply and prices controlled by suppliers outside the UK
Coal	Greenhouse gases and particulates Contributes to acid rain	Large stocks underground in the UK
Wind	Expensive to build Variable output	No greenhouse gases Plenty of windy locations in the UK and at sea
Hydroelectric	Need to build dams and flood land Expensive	Limited suitable locations No greenhouse gases
Solar	Needs a large surface area due to low average sunlight intensities in the UK Expensive	Can be used to supplement other energy supplies Can be placed on roofs so unobtrusive
Nuclear	Dealing with radioactive waste	Clean fuel with high energy output Comes from stable regions of the world

Three ministers are discussing the future energy needs of the UK.

Minister A says: "There is only a need for gas. It is cheaper than the others, doesn't produce solid waste and the power stations don't cover as much land as the alternative energy sources do."

Minister B says: "I would only use solar energy or wind power as they are green energy sources and are friendly to the environment."

Minister C says: "You can't just rely on one energy source. There are problems with the alternative energy sources, although they can play their part."

(a) For each of Minister B's choices of energy source, give **one** reason why relying only on them is not a good idea. [2]

Solar energy: ....

....

Wind power: ....

....

(b) Minister A's argument is that the only source of energy needed is gas. Give **one** reason, using the information in the table, why this is not a good idea. [1]

....

....

(c) Minister C mentions that more than one energy source is needed and alternative energy sources can play their part. Explain how alternative energy sources could play their part in providing energy for homes and industry, and why it is important to have more than one energy source.

✏ *The quality of written communication will be assessed in your answer to this question.* [6]

....

....

....

....

....

....

16. This question is about the use of electrical appliances.

Michael is doing some DIY on his home.

(a) He needs to lift a 2000N pallet of bricks 5m from the ground floor to the upstairs balcony. The electric motor takes 25 seconds to do the job. What is the rate at which the motor transfers energy? [2]

....

.... J/s *or* W

P3 Sustainable Energy

(b) Michael uses a 230V electric drill to make a hole in the wall for a lamp fitting. The drill is rated at 1150W.

  (i) What current will the drill use from the mains? [2]

  .... amps

  (ii) If the job takes 3 minutes, how much energy, in joules, is transferred? [2]

  .... joules

  (iii) How many units of electricity (kilowatt hours) does the job use? [2]

  .... kWh

  (iv) If the cost of electricity is 8p per kilowatt hour, what will the cost of the electricity used for the job be? [2]

  .... p

(c) At the end of the day, Michael switches on his washing machine. The efficiency of the motor in the washing machine is 65%. The input power to the motor is 2kW.

  (i) What is the useful power output? [2]

  .... W

  (ii) How much useful work will the motor do in 5 minutes? [2]

  .... joules

  [Total: .... / 23]

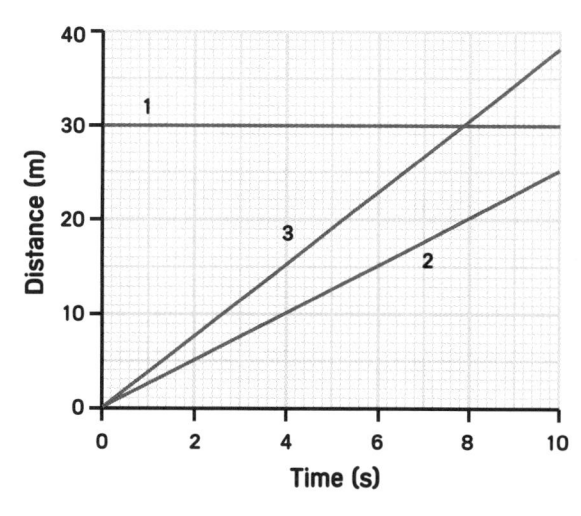

Explaining Motion P4

1. **(a) (i)** Jenny, Amelia, Samantha and Ann have a race to see who can run the fastest. Which sprinter has the greatest average speed? Put a tick (✓) in the box next to the correct answer. [1]

   Jenny ran 100m in 15 seconds. ☐   Amelia ran 80m in 12 seconds. ☐

   Samantha ran 150m in 20 seconds. ☐   Ann ran 60m in 17 seconds. ☐

   (ii) Calculate the average speed of a runner who runs a 1200m race in 150 seconds. [2]

   ....

   .... m/s

   (iii) Why is the speed calculated called the average speed? [1]

   ....

   (iv) What does the term **instantaneous speed** mean? [1]

   ....

   (b) How is the **velocity** of an object different from its speed? [1]

   ....

   (c) What does the term **acceleration** mean? [1]

   ....

2. Put a ring around the correct options in the following sentences. [4]

   The **height / gradient** of a distance–time graph is a measure of the **speed / acceleration** of the object.

   The steeper the slope, the **faster / slower** the object is moving. The motion of a stationary object is

   represented by a **horizontal / vertical** line.

3. The graph shows the motion of three objects.

P4 Explaining Motion

Put a tick (✓) in the correct box to show whether each statement is **true** or **false**. [4]

		true	false
(a)	Object 2 is moving more quickly than object 3.	☐	☐
(b)	Object 3 is moving at a greater speed than object 1.	☐	☐
(c)	Object 1 is stationary.	☐	☐
(d)	Objects 2 and 3 are both accelerating.	☐	☐

4. Plot distance–time graphs to represent the following:

   (a) Colin standing stationary 5m from a starting point (O). [1]

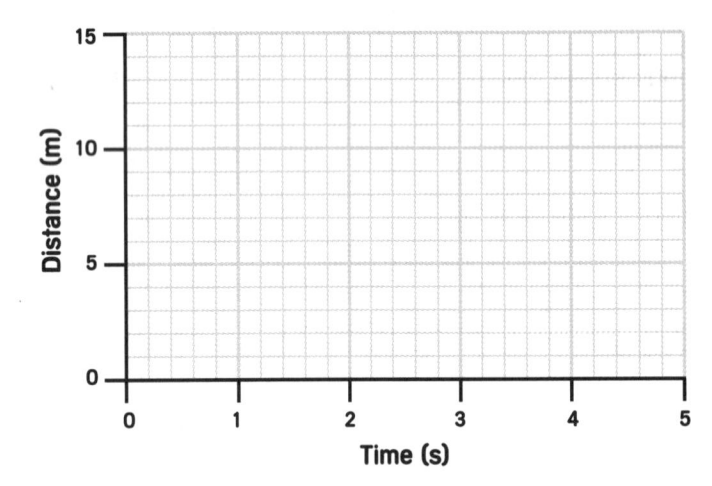

   (b) Alice running at a constant speed of 5m/s. [1]

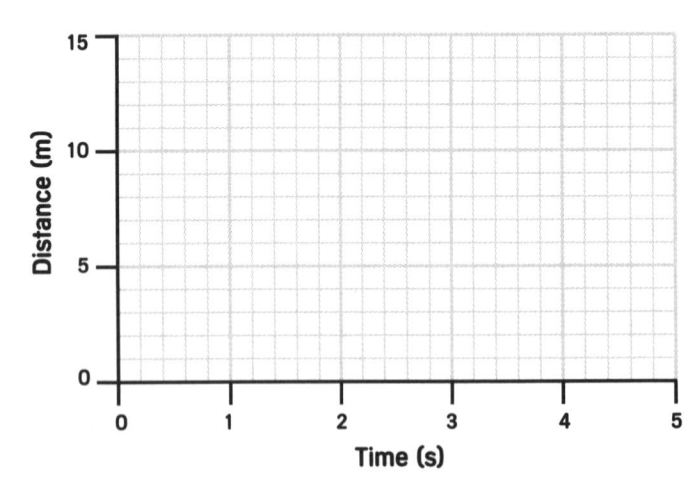

5. (a) Put a ring around the correct options in the following sentences. [4]

   The **height / gradient** of a speed–time graph is the **speed / acceleration** of the object. The steeper the slope, the more **quickly / slowly** the object is accelerating. The motion of an object moving with constant speed is represented by a **horizontal / vertical** line.

Explaining Motion — P4

(b) On the grid provided, mark the following points. [3]

   (i) Point **A** where the object is stationary

   (ii) Point **B** where the object is moving at a constant speed

   (iii) Point **C** where the object is accelerating

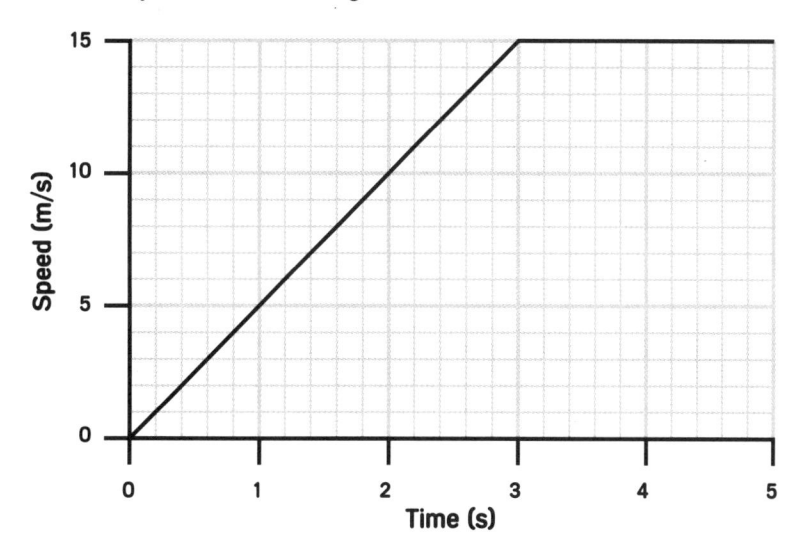

[Graph: Speed (m/s) vs Time (s). Line rises from (0,0) to (3,15) then remains horizontal at 15 m/s to (5,15).]

6. (a) What **two** things do you need to know to work out the acceleration of an object? [1]

.... and ....

(b) What units are used to measure acceleration? Put a tick (✓) in the box next to the correct answer. [1]

Metres per second (m/s) ☐   Metres per second² (m/s²) ☐

Miles per hour (mph) ☐   Kilometres per hour (km/h) ☐

(c) (i) Jane accelerates her car uniformly from rest to a speed of 15m/s in a time of 5 seconds. Calculate the acceleration of the car. [2]

(ii) Harry is a train driver. He accelerates his train from a speed of 20m/s to 34m/s in 4 seconds. Calculate the acceleration of the train. [2]

(iii) Matt is a fighter pilot. After travelling at a speed of 40m/s, he lands on an aircraft carrier where he stops. The descent takes 2 seconds. Calculate the deceleration of the plane. [2]

P4 Explaining Motion

7. The table shows the speed and time of a motorcyclist for the first 20 seconds of her journey.

Time (s)	0	2	4	6	8	10	12	14	16	18	20
Speed (m/s)	0	5	10	10	10	12	14	14	15	16	16

(a) Label the axes below and plot a speed–time graph of the motorcyclist's journey on the grid below. [3]

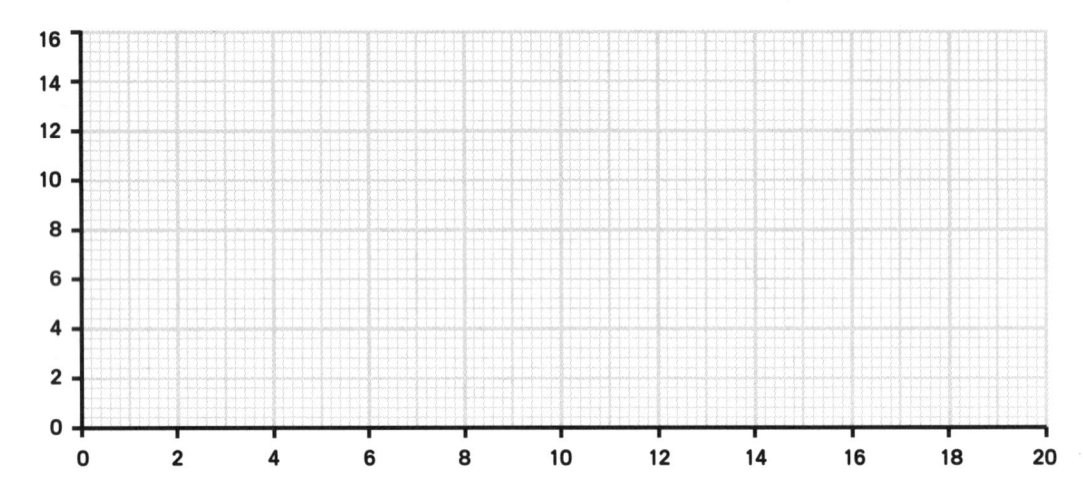

(b) Calculate the following:

   (i) The acceleration of the bike in the first 4 seconds. [2]

   ....

   .... m/s^2

   (ii) The acceleration of the bike after 8 seconds until it reaches a speed of 14m/s. [2]

   ....

   .... m/s^2

(c) The total distance travelled was 228m. Calculate the average speed for the whole journey. [2]

   ....

   .... m/s

Explaining Motion P4

8. **(a)** Complete the table with the names and descriptions of four forces. [4]

Name of Force	Description of Force
	Acts to slow things down when two surfaces rub against each other
Air resistance	
	Pushes up on the bottom of a cup sitting on a table and stops the cup sinking into the table
Gravity	

(b) Whenever something exerts a force, it experiences an equal and opposite force. Explain how this principle is used in jet engines.

The quality of written communication will be assessed in your answer to this question. [6]

(c) Give **two** examples of how friction can be useful and explain how each one works. [4]

1.

2.

P4 Explaining Motion

9. **(a)** What **two** things are represented by an arrow on a force diagram? Put ticks (✓) in the boxes next to the **two** correct statements. [2]

- The size of the force ☐
- The type of force ☐
- The name of the force ☐
- The direction of the force ☐

(b) What is meant by the term **resultant force**? [2]

....

....

(c) The following diagrams show a car travelling at 30km/h. Calculate the resultant force and state how it affects the car's motion, if at all.

(i) 1000N ← car → 4000N

.... [2]

(ii) 2000N ← car → 0N

.... [2]

(iii) 1000N ← car → 1000N

.... [2]

(d) Calculate the size of the resultant force in each case, stating the direction.

(i) 2N ← □ → 4N, with 1N up and 1N down

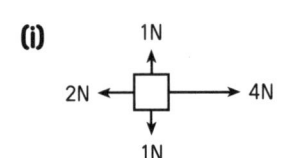

.... [2]

(ii) 5N up, 2N down, 7N left, 3N left, 4N right, 6N right

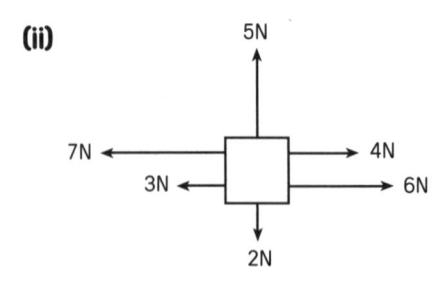

.... [2]

40 © Lonsdale

Explaining Motion P4

(e) A car travelling at 40km/h in a 20km/h zone hits a pedestrian and injures him. Three bystanders make the following observations.

Noah
If the car had been travelling at the speed limit, there may not have been an accident.

Anna
The fact that the driver was speeding means that the pedestrian had no chance of avoiding the accident.

Bob
There are too many uncontrolled factors to come to a conclusion.

(i) Who is suggesting that there is a correlation between speeding and the chance of having an accident? [1]

(ii) Who is suggesting the speeding car caused the accident? [1]

(iii) Who is suggesting a fair test? [1]

10. Caitlin jumps out of a plane. She does not initially open her parachute but freefalls towards the ground. As she falls, she accelerates.

(a) Look at the diagrams of Caitlin as she falls. They are not in the correct order. Put the letters in the empty boxes to show the correct order. [3]

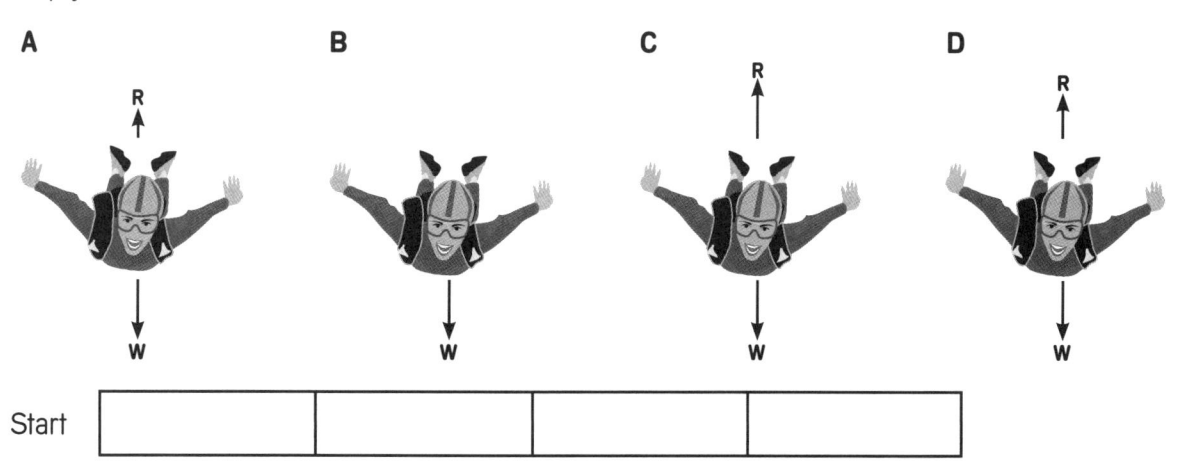

A   B   C   D

Start

P4 Explaining Motion

(b) The speed–time graph shows how Caitlin's speed changes after she jumps out of the plane.

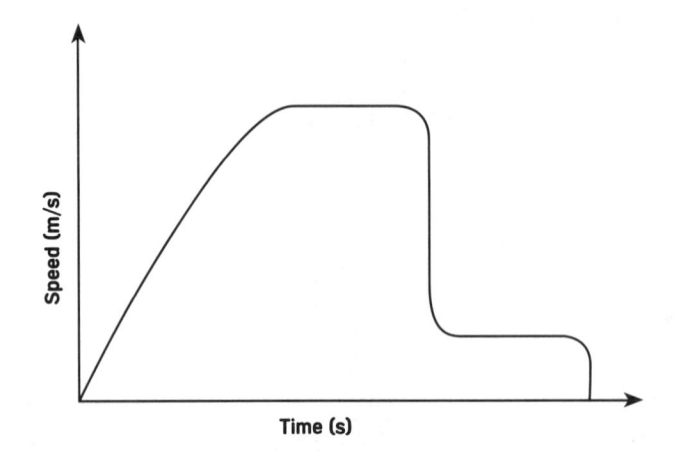

[Speed (m/s) vs Time (s) graph]

Explain the shape of the graph by describing how the forces acting on Caitlin change as she falls.

✎ *The quality of written communication will be assessed in your answer to this question.* [6]

11. (a) Which object has the greatest momentum? Put a tick (✓) in the box next to the correct answer. [1]

A lorry travelling at 50mph ☐   A car travelling at 50mph ☐

(b) Complete the following sentences. Use words from this list. [3]

    change   **not change**   **acceleration**   **mass**
    velocity   **stationary**

If the resultant force acting on an object is zero its momentum will ....

An object's momentum can be increased by increasing its .... or by

increasing its ....

Explaining Motion — P4

12. Complete the following table. [4]

Momentum (kg m/s)	Mass (kg)	Velocity (m/s)
	50	10
	1000	30
3000		30
800	400	

13. Explain how a crumple zone is used in cars as a safety feature.

The quality of written communication will be assessed in your answer to this question. [6]

14. A student investigates how kinetic energy depends on speed. He has a tape measure, a stopwatch, an electronic balance and a small trolley.

(a) Describe what measurements he needs to make to calculate the trolley's kinetic energy. [3]

(b) This graph shows the results:

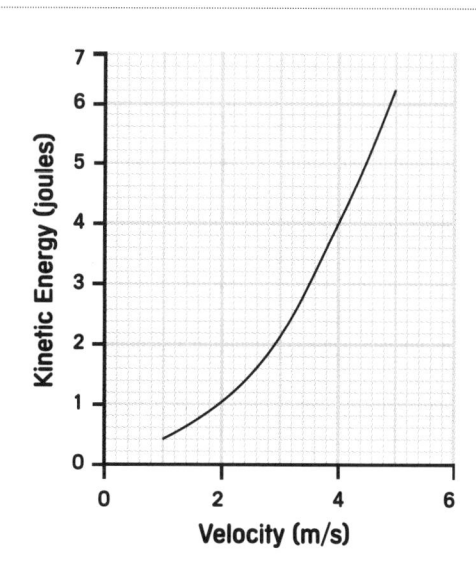

P4 Explaining Motion

(i) Use the graph to find the kinetic energy at a velocity of 2m/s and 4m/s. [2]

(ii) Describe the trend shown by the graph. [2]

(iii) Extend the graph to show how kinetic energy changes as the velocity reduces to zero and explain why. [2]

15. (a) Which object will have more gravitational potential energy? Put a tick (✓) in the box next to the correct answer in each part. [2]

   (i) A pendulum at the top of its swing ☐   A pendulum at the bottom of its swing ☐

   (ii) A cyclist at the bottom of a hill ☐   A cyclist at the top of a hill ☐

   (b) Complete the following sentences. Use words from this list. [2]

   chemical   electrical   gravitational   kinetic

   As a sledge is pulled up a hill it gains _____ potential energy. As it starts to slide down the hill the energy is turned into _____ energy.

   (c) Calculate the gain in gravitational potential energy of a climber with a weight of 500N who climbs up a cliff 100m high. Include the units in your answer. [3]

16. Gill pushes her bike home from school a distance of 500m. It takes a force of 10N to overcome the forces of friction. Calculate the amount of work she will have done to get her bike home. Include the units in your answer. [3]

[Total: _____ / 114]

Explaining Motion — P4

Higher Tier

17. The displacement–time graph shows the journey of a ball being kicked against a wall.

(a) What is the average velocity of this journey? [2]

.... m/s

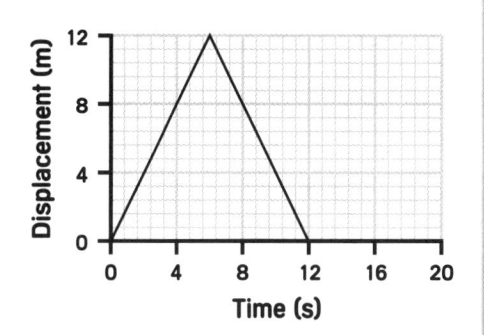

(b) What is the average speed of this journey? [2]

.... m/s

(c) Calculate the speed for the first part of the journey. [2]

.... m/s

(d) On a distance–time graph, what would a curved line indicate? [1]

....

18. (a) Complete the following sentences. Use words from this list. [3]

constant   changing   speeding up   slowing down   stationary

On a distance–time graph, if the motion of an object is represented by a curved line, then the speed of the object is .... If the gradient is increasing, the object is .... If the gradient is decreasing, then the object is ....

(b) The graph shows a runner's journey. What is the average speed of this journey? [2]

.... m/s

P4 Explaining Motion

19. Alex is practising driving his car. The velocity–time graph shows his journey. Describe the motion of the car during each stage of the journey.

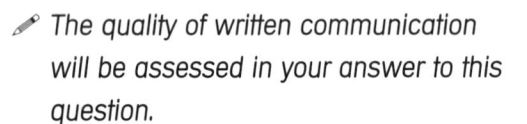

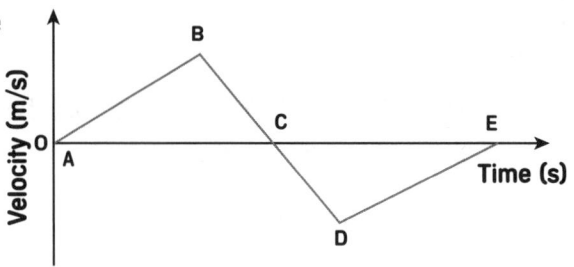

✏️ *The quality of written communication will be assessed in your answer to this question.* [6]

20. Tina was riding her bike to the shops from her house. She travelled at 5m/s for 20 seconds, then gradually slowed down over 10 seconds to come to rest at the shop 130m from the start position.

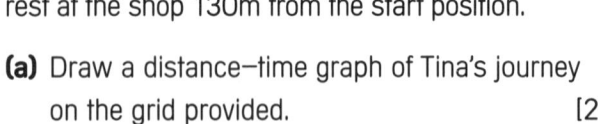

(a) Draw a distance–time graph of Tina's journey on the grid provided. [2]

(b) On her way back from the shops, Tina stops to talk to a friend 20m away from the shops. What is Tina's displacement from her house? [1]

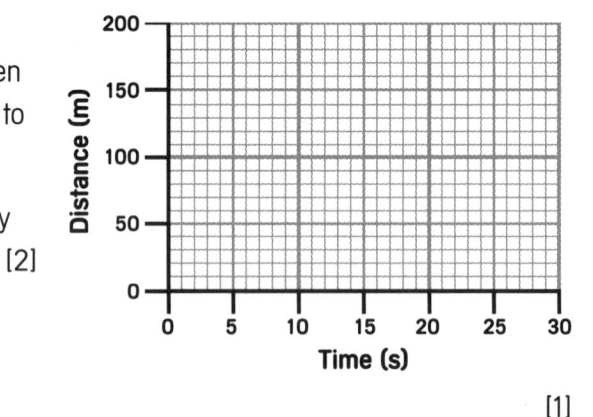

.... m

(c) Tina and her bike have a combined mass of 70kg. At one point in her journey she and her bike have kinetic energy of 560J. The formula for calculating kinetic energy is:

Kinetic energy = $\frac{1}{2}$ × Mass × Velocity^2

Use the formula to calculate Tina's velocity. Include units in your answer. [3]

[Total: .... / 24]

Electric Circuits P5

1. Complete the following sentences. Use words from this list. You may use them more than once. [5]

    current   **linear**   **related**   **unchanged**
        voltage   **correlation**   **halved**
       resistance   **proportional**   **doubled**

The graph shows how the _____ through a resistor changes

as the _____ across the resistor changes. The straight line

tells you that the current is _____ to the

_____ across the resistor. So if the value of the voltage

is doubled, the current flowing is _____ .

2. This question is about static electricity.

(a) When a plastic rod is rubbed with a cloth, the rod becomes positively charged. Which of the statements below is correct? Put a tick (✓) in the box next to the correct statement. [1]

The rod is positively charged because it has gained electrons. ◯

Protons have been rubbed off the cloth onto the rod. ◯

The rod has lost electrons. ◯

The cloth has lost electrons to the rod. ◯

(b) When aeroplanes fly through the air, they can become charged. They need to be discharged on landing by an earth wire. Which of the statements below are correct? Put ticks (✓) in the boxes next to the **three** correct statements. [3]

The earth wire is an insulator. ◯

Positive ions will move up the wire to cancel out the electrons. ◯

There are free electrons in the wire to allow a current to flow. ◯

A current will flow in the wire. ◯

The resistance of the wire is large. ◯

Some energy in the wire will be lost as heat on discharge. ◯

(c) A person rubs a Perspex rod with a cloth and the Perspex rod becomes negatively charged. The rod is then suspended from a clamp stand using insulated string. Another Perspex rod, which has also been rubbed with the same type of cloth, is brought near to it. Describe what will happen. [1]

_____

P5 Electric Circuits

3. This question is about components in a series circuit. The diagram shows a series circuit containing two resistors, R₁ and R₂, powered by a battery.

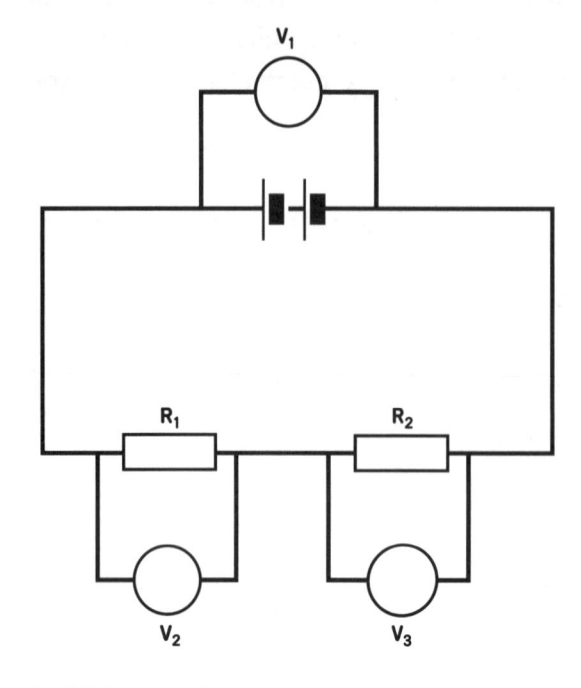

(a) (i) If voltmeter V₁ reads 20V and voltmeter V₃ reads 8V, what will be the reading on voltmeter V₂? [2]

....

.... volts

(ii) If a current of 2A flows in the circuit and voltmeter V₃ reads 8V, what will be the value of the resistance R₁? [2]

....

.... Ω

(b) Resistor R₁ is replaced in the circuit by a resistor of 16Ω. Voltmeter V₃ now reads 4V. The reading on voltmeter V₁ remains 20V.

(i) What current would now flow in the circuit? [2]

....

.... amps

(ii) How much work is done when 3 units of charge (coulombs) flow through the 16Ω resistor? [2]

....

.... joules

Electric Circuits   P5

(c) Resistor R₂ is replaced by a thermistor. The current flowing is measured as 0.5A. The resistance of R₁ is 16Ω. V₁ still reads 20V.

Explain what would happen in the circuit if the thermistor was placed into a beaker of ice.

You will need to consider what will happen to the resistance of the thermistor and how that would alter the current flowing in the circuit. You should also consider what changes might occur to the readings shown on the voltmeters.

The quality of written communication will be assessed in your answer to this question. [6]

---

4. Complete the following sentences. Use words from this list. [4]

> volts   charge   used   amps   conductors
> not used   positive ions   insulators   protons

An electric current is a flow of .... It is measured in ....

Metals are .... as there are lots of charges free to move. A battery can make

these charges move and they are .... up as they flow around a circuit.

5. Wasim sets up the circuit shown in the diagram. When he closes the switch, the resistor gets hot. Explain why that happens. [4]

Switch

P5 Electric Circuits

6. A group of students is discussing moving magnets in coils of wire.

Chevelle: When I move a magnet towards a coil of wire, a voltage is induced across the coil.

Toni: The faster I move the magnet towards the coil, the larger the induced voltage.

Jason: If I wrap the coil of wire around a piece of copper, then move the magnet towards the coil, I will get a bigger voltage than before.

Yvonne: If I reverse the magnet, the induced voltage will also be reversed when I move the magnet towards the coil.

(a) Which student is making an incorrect statement? [1]

(b) Which student is talking about the rate at which field lines are cut? [1]

7. This question is about the motor effect.

The diagram shows a wire carrying a current placed in a magnetic field.

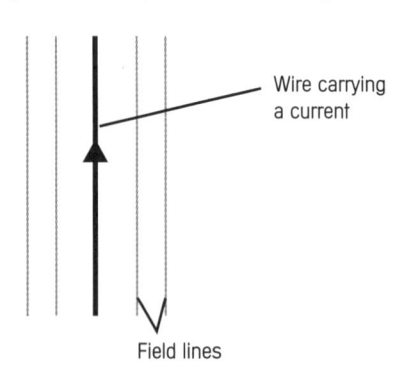

OCR Twenty First Century GCSE Physics A Workbook Answers

Answering Quality of Written Communication Questions

A number of the questions in your examinations will include an assessment of the quality of your written communication (QWC). These questions are worth a maximum of 6 marks and are indicated by a pencil icon.

Your answers to these questions will be marked according to...
- the level of your understanding of the relevant science
- how well you structure your answer
- the style of your writing, including the quality of your punctuation, grammar and spelling.

QWC questions will be marked using a 'Levels of Response' mark scheme. The examiner will decide whether your answer is in the top level, middle level or bottom level. The expected quality of written communication is different in the three levels and it will always be considered at the same time as looking at the scientific information in your answer:
- To achieve Level 3 (which is the top level and is worth 5–6 marks), your answer should contain relevant science, and be organised and presented in a structured and coherent manner. You should use scientific terms appropriately and your spelling, punctuation and grammar should have very few errors.
- For Level 2 (worth 3–4 marks), there may be more errors in your spelling, punctuation and grammar, and your answer will miss some of the things expected at Level 3.

- For Level 1 (worth 1–2 marks), your answer may be written using simplistic language. You will have included some relevant science, but the quality of your written communication may have limited how well the examiner can understand your answer. This could be due to lots of errors in spelling, punctuation and grammar, misuse of scientific terms or a poor structure.
- An answer given Level 0 may contain insufficient or irrelevant science, and will not be given any marks.

You will be awarded the higher or lower mark within a particular level depending on the quality of the science and the quality of the written communication in your answer.

Even if the quality of your written communication is perfect, the level you are awarded will be limited if you show little understanding of the relevant science, and you will be given Level 0 if you show no relevant scientific understanding at all.

To help you understand the criteria above, three specimen answers are provided to the first QWC question in this workbook. The first is a model answer worth 6 marks, the second answer would be worth 4 marks and the third answer worth 2 marks. The three exemplar answers are differentiated by their scientific content and use of scientific terminology. Model answers worth 6 marks are provided to all other QWC questions to help you aspire to the best possible marks.

Module P1: The Earth in the Universe (Pages 3–13)

1. (a) 4500 million years ago **should be ticked**.
    (b) **Any suitable answers, e.g.** There was no way of testing it; It was an old, established theory.

2. (a) 5(m)
    (b) Frequency = Speed ÷ Wavelength
        = 4 ÷ 10
        = 0.4(Hz)
        [1 for correct working but wrong answer]

3. (a) The theory of continental drift states that the continents were once joined together **[1]** but became separated and drifted apart **[1]**.
    (b) **This is a model answer which would score full marks:** Wegener saw that all the continents fitted together like a jigsaw, especially the coastlines of South America and Africa. Sedimentary rock formations in South America and Africa matched up. Also, fossils of the same land animals were found on different continents as well as living land animals today. Wegener's theory was rejected by many scientists because he wasn't a geologist and was treated as an outsider. The movement of the continents was not measurable at that time and a land bridge between continents provided a more likely explanation. Modern evidence of continental drift is provided by magnetic striping either side of the Mid-Atlantic Ridge as the seafloor spreads by a few centimetres each year.
    This answer would score 4 marks: Wegener saw that all the continents fitted together like a jigsaw. Rock formations on different continents matched up. The fossil record is similar on different continents. Wegener's theory was rejected as the movement of continents couldn't be measured at that time. Modern evidence is magnetic striping on the seafloor.
    This answer would score 2 marks: Wegener saw that all the continents fitted together like a jigsaw. Rock formations and fossils matched on different continents. There was too little evidence for Wegener's theory at that time.

4. (a) Tectonic plates **should be ticked**.
    (b) Earthquakes; Volcanoes; Mountain formations
    (c) liquid; Convection; tectonic; magma

5. Slide past each other; Move apart; Move towards each other (destructive)

6. (a) Plates sliding past each other
    (b) **Any two from:** At a constructive plate boundary the tectonic plates move apart; Molten rock rises to the surface, where it solidifies to form new rock (seafloor spreading); The process is driven by convection currents in the mantle.
        1 mark for a suitable example, e.g. Oceanic ridges such as the Mid-Atlantic Ridge; the Rift Valley in Africa
    (c) **Any two from:** At a destructive plate boundary the tectonic plates move towards each other; One plate is forced under the other plate / The thinner, denser oceanic plate is forced under the thicker continental plate; Earthquakes and volcanoes are common.
        1 mark for a suitable example, e.g. The west coast of South America
    (d) The oceanic plate is forced under the continental plate; Melting / Subduction occurs
    (e) Tectonic plates are less dense than the mantle and therefore float on top **should be ticked**.

7. (a) gas; gravity; heat; fusion
    (b) **Lines should be drawn from** Asteroids **to** Small rocky masses that orbit the Sun; **from** Comets **to** Small icy masses that orbit the Sun; **from** Dwarf planets **to** Large masses that have not cleared their orbits of other objects; **from** Moons **to** Rocky masses that orbit planets; **and from** Planets **to** Large masses that orbit the Sun. **[1 for each correct line up to a maximum of 4.]**
    (c) | B | C | A | E | D |
    [1 for each correctly placed up to a maximum of 4.]

8. (a) About 5000 million years old
    (b) Energy is released during the process of nuclear fusion **[1]**. Lighter elements such as hydrogen atoms fuse to make new heavier elements such as helium **[1]**.
    (c) Our galaxy contains at least 100 billion stars **should be ticked**.
    (d) | B | C | D | E | A |
    [1 for each correctly placed up to a maximum of 4.]
    (e) A light-year is the distance light travels in one year **[1]** (approximately 9500 billion kilometres). Scientists use light-years to measure distances in space because they are so vast **[1]**.
    (f) The light we see today left the galaxy 2.2 million years ago **[1]**. We are therefore seeing the galaxy as it was in the past **[1]**.
    (g) Relative brightness; Parallax

9. **Any three from:** Visible light; Ultraviolet; Infrared; Gamma; X-rays; Microwave; Radio

10. Light pollution is the effect of the electric lights that illuminate the night sky and make it difficult to see the stars.

11. (a) That the Universe started with a huge explosion
    (b) 14 000 million years

12. (a) energy; matter; energy; travels
    (b) (i) For a longitudinal wave the pattern of disturbance is in the same direction as the direction of the wave movement **[1]**, while for a transverse wave the pattern of disturbance is at right angles to the direction of wave movement **[1]**.
        (ii) Longitudinal: sound waves; Transverse: light / water waves
    (c) (i) The number of waves produced / passing a particular point in one second
        (ii) Hertz

13. (a) Robert
    (b) There is a very large number of hydrogen nuclei **[1]** and therefore the total amount of energy released is very large **[1]**.
    (c) **This is a model answer which would score full marks:**
    All stars have a finite life span. They obtain their energy from converting hydrogen into helium in nuclear fusion. Eventually hydrogen supplies run out and they begin to convert helium into heavier elements, such as carbon and lithium. Massive stars eventually explode in a supernova during which the very heavy elements, such as gold, are formed.

14. (a) **and and but not should be ringed**.
    (b) (i) All the points, A, B, C, D, E, F and G
        (ii) A, B, F and G
    (c) Waves are refracted gradually **[1]** because they change speed as the density changes gradually **[1]**.
    (d) Waves are refracted suddenly **[1]** at a change in material, where their speed changes suddenly **[1]**.

15. **This is a model answer which would score full marks:**
    The Earth has a magnetic field. The polarity of the field changes approximately every one million years. New rock is formed at constructive plate boundaries where the plates are moving apart. As the rock cools, the polarity of the Earth's magnetic field is set in the solid rock. This produces stripes of alternating polarity. Geologists can use this to estimate how quickly new rock is formed and therefore how quickly tectonic plates are moving. An example would be the Mid-Atlantic Ridge.

16. **This is a model answer which would score full marks:**
    Tectonic plates move due to convection currents in the mantle. Old rock is destroyed through subduction. Igneous rock is formed when magma reaches the surface. Plate collisions produce high pressure and temperatures, which can cause folding and change sedimentary rock into metamorphic rock.

17. Most galaxies appear to be red shifted and the more distant a galaxy is, the more it is red shifted, which means that they are moving away from us **[1]**. If they are moving away from us, then the Universe is expanding **[1]**.

18. (a) The amount of mass in the Universe.
    (b) 'Big crunch': Too much mass
    Expand forever: Not enough mass

19. (a) **Lines should be drawn from** P-wave **to** Longitudinal **and from** S-wave **to** Transverse.
    (b) The speed is greater in the mantle because it is denser than the crust **[1]**. Mechanical waves travel more quickly through denser materials **[1]** as the particles are closer together and the vibrations are passed on more quickly **[1]**.
    (c) P-wave: time = 40 ÷ 6 = 6.7(s)
    S-wave, time = 40 ÷ 4 = 10(s)
    10 − 6.7 = 3.3(s)
    [All correct for 3 marks; 1 for correct working but wrong answer]

Module P2: Radiation and Life
(Pages 14–23)

1. (a) Photons **should be ticked**.
    (b) Microwaves: **D**; Infrared: **C**; X-rays: **B**; Gamma rays: **A [1 for each correct up to a maximum of 3.]**

2. (a) **Any four suitable pairs, e.g.** Emitter: Sun, Detector: The eye; Emitter: Remote control, Detector: Television; Emitter: Stars, Detector: Gamma ray telescope; Emitter: X-ray machine, Detector: Photographic plate **[1 for each correct pair.]**
    (b) reflected; absorbed; transmitted **[1 for each correct up to a maximum of 2.]**

3. (a) Increase the distance between the source and the object; Place a material which absorbs the radiation between the source and the object.
    (b) The number of photons; The energy of each photon

4. (a) Tom; Jack
    (b) Anna
    (c) Grace; Emily

5. Ionising radiation can break molecules into bits called ions **and** X-rays and gamma rays are types of ionising radiation **should be ticked**.

6. (a) Surrounding nuclear reactors with lead **and** Wire screens in microwave ovens **should be ticked**.
    (b) Ionising radiation can damage cells; Ionising radiation can cause mutations which can lead to cancer.
    (c) By causing the water particles **[1]** in materials to vibrate **[1]**

7. (a) More heat will be absorbed by the atmosphere **should be ticked**.
    (b) photosynthesis; decreases **and** increases **should be ringed**.

8. (a) Less heat escapes back into space
    (b) Methane; Carbon dioxide; Water vapour

9. **This is a model answer which would score full marks:**
Ozone is part of the atmosphere. The ozone layer absorbs some of the ultraviolet radiation from the Sun before it reaches the Earth. Ultraviolet radiation can be harmful if too much reaches the Earth's surface as it increases the risk of skin cancer.

10. (a) Eating of plants: D; Photosynthesis: B; Respiration: A; Death of plants and animals: C **[1 for each correct up to a maximum of 3.]**
    (b) Photosynthesis **[1]** by plants **[1]**
    (c) **This is a model answer which would score full marks:**
    The carbon obtained by photosynthesis is used to make carbohydrates, fats and proteins in plants. When the plants are eaten by animals, this carbon becomes carbohydrates, fats and proteins in the animals. Animals respire, releasing carbon dioxide back into the atmosphere.
    (d) The amount of carbon dioxide added to the atmosphere (by burning, respiration, etc. **[1]** was roughly the same as the amount of carbon dioxide removed from the atmosphere by the process of photosynthesis **[1]**.
    (e) **This is a model answer which would score full marks:**
    Burning fossil fuels releases previously trapped carbon dioxide into the atmosphere. Deforestation is the removal of trees and this decreases the amount of carbon dioxide that is taken out of the atmosphere by photosynthesis.

11. (a) They have higher energy **and** They are not significantly refracted by the atmosphere **should be ticked**.
    (b) (i) X-rays
        (ii) Radio waves
        (iii) Microwaves
        (iv) **Any one from:** Light; Infrared
    (c) X-rays are absorbed by dense materials but can travel through less dense materials **[1]**. X-rays can cause changes in photographic film **[1]**.

12. (a) Frequency **and** Amplitude **should be ticked**.
    (b) A receiver decodes the pattern of variation **[1]** and reproduces the original sound **[1]**.

13. (a) An analogue signal can take any value, whereas a digital signal can only take two values, 0 or 1.
    (b) (i) False
        (ii) True
        (iii) True
        (iv) True
    (c) (i)

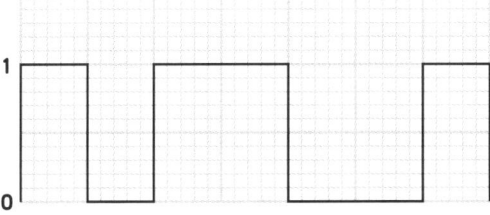

    [1 for graph involving only vertical and horizontal lines; 1 for correct pattern of 0 and 1. Any height for the value of 1 and any width can be used so long as they are constant.]
    (ii) Any suitable answer, e.g.

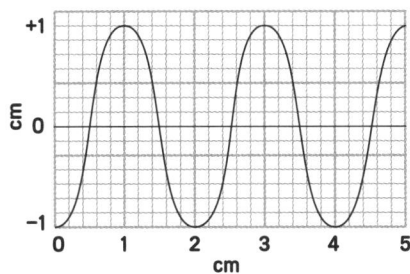

    [1 for correct wavelength (2cm on horizontal axis for one complete wave); 1 for correct amplitude (1cm on vertical axis from the undisturbed position to *either* a peak *or* a trough)]

    (d) Unwanted electrical interference
    (e) A received analogue signal

14. Photons spread out; Photons are absorbed by particles; Photons are reflected by particles.

15. **Any one from:** duration; time

16. very reactive **and** can **should be ringed**.

17. (a) **Any two from:** Apply sun lotion; Wear clothing that covers the skin; Stay indoors
    (b) Sunburn and skin cancer

18. (a) Computer climate models **[1]** show that one of the main factors responsible for global warming is the rise in atmospheric carbon dioxide and other greenhouse gases **[1]**. This increase is caused by human activity such as deforestation **[1]**. **[Any suitable example can be given for 1 mark.]**
    (b) **This is a model answer which would score full marks:**
    Burning forests increases the amount of carbon dioxide in the atmosphere. This is because combustion releases carbon dioxide more quickly than respiration and natural decomposition would. Also, photosynthesis by plants absorbs carbon dioxide from the atmosphere, so their removal means that less carbon dioxide is absorbed.

19. (a) **This is a model answer which would score full marks:**
    Digital signals have two states, on and off, which can still be recognised despite any noise that is picked up. Therefore, it is easy to remove the noise / clean up the signal / restore the on/off pattern. Analogue signals have many different values, so it is hard to distinguish between noise and the original signal. This means that the noise cannot be completely removed and when the signal is amplified, any noise picked up is also amplified.
    (b) (i) Both
        (ii) Digital
        (iii) Digital
        (iv) Analogue

Module P3: Sustainable Energy
(Pages 24–34)

1. (a) A magnet **[1]** rotates near a coil **[1]**.
   (b) (i) Potential energy; PE to kinetic energy; KE to Electrical **[All three needed for 2 marks. 1 mark for 'KE to Electrical'.]**
       (ii) Current = Power rating in watts ÷ Voltage
       = 36 ÷ 12 = 3(amps)
       [1 for correct working but wrong answer]
       (iii) Energy used = Power rating × Time in seconds
       = 36 × 20 × 60 = 43 200 (joules)
       [1 for correct working but wrong answer]
   (c) (i) Cindy
       (ii) Alex

2. (a) Electrical **should be ticked**.
   (b) It has to be produced from another (primary) energy source.

3. (a) Coal:
   Any one from: Emission of carbon dioxide; Emission of sulfur dioxide; Emission of particulates; Contributes to global warming / climate change; Not renewable
   Nuclear power:
   Any one from: Disposal of nuclear waste; Possibility of radioactive contamination; Perceived threat to the public; Power stations need a water supply
   (b) **This is a model answer which would score full marks:**
   Two possible alternative energy sources are wind and wave. Neither of these alternative sources emit any greenhouse gases or any gases that cause acid rain. Nor do they release particulates into the atmosphere. They are both renewable sources of energy. Neither generates nuclear

waste, which is hazardous to both process and dispose of safely, nor do they emit radiation which can cause damage to living cells.
[Coastal areas are typical sites for tidal, wave and wind for obvious reasons, so these should be expected to be seen as answers with the advantages stated as above. Hydroelectric is unlikely to be suitable, as valleys that can be dammed are not necessarily near the coast. Solar is not necessarily suitable as it depends on the latitude of the location. Biomass requires large land area for production and coastal areas are usually prime real estate, so it would be very expensive to use land for biomass. Inland sites would be better. Geothermal is very dependent on location, so the coast is not necessarily the best place.]

4. (a) Heat
   (b) 5%
   (c) **Any one from:** Gas; Coal; Oil
   (d) 55J **should be ringed**.

5. Energy is released from the nucleus. Heat is used to produce steam. Steam turns a turbine. The turbine drives the generator **should be ticked**.

6. Drawing a larger current from the generator would use up more petrol each second **should be ticked**.

7. **Lines should be drawn from** Wind farm **to** Are there any hills to cause turbulence?; **from** Biofuel **to** Is there sufficient farmland available?; **and from** Hydroelectric power **to** Is there a suitable place for a dam?
   [1 for each correct line up to a maximum of 2.]

8. (a) Use of more efficient appliances; Installation of loft insulation
   (b) Saving by use of more efficient appliances (condensing boiler) = 3 × £190 = £570
   Saving by installation of loft insulation = 3 × £145 = £435
   Total savings = £570 + £435 = £1005
   [1 for correct working but wrong answer]
   (c) **Any one from:** There is less wasted energy in the form of heat to pay for when using low energy bulbs; Low energy bulbs need to be replaced less often than normal ones.
   (d) **This is a model answer which would score full marks:**
   New products are made from raw materials and require energy to be used at each stage of the manufacturing process. Recycling will cut down on the number of new products required and therefore saves energy. Also, there will be less money spent and less energy wasted on disposal to landfill sites.

9. Supplies of coal from British mines ran out in the 1990s **and** The use of hydroelectric power increased after 1990 due to increased rainfall **should be ticked**.

10. (a) Units used in kWh = Power rating × Time
    = 0.1 × 8 = 0.8kWh
    Cost = Units used in kWh × Cost per unit
    = 0.8 × 8 = 6.4p
    [1 for correct working but wrong answer]
    (b) Efficiency = Useful energy transferred ÷ Energy in × 100%
    = 1800 ÷ 3000 × 100% = 60%
    [1 for correct working but wrong answer]

11. (a) (i) Any suitable answer, e.g. People changed from using coal (fires) to gas (central heating). **['Gas was a more convenient source of energy than coal, which had to be stored on site' is also acceptable.]**
    (ii) The mass of coal mined has remained constant since 2000.
    (b) There is no data for the years in between the ones on the chart, so conclusions are made on limited information.

12. **This is a model answer which would score full marks:**
    Biofuels and solar panels would both require large areas of land to produce sufficient energy. Burning biofuels also leads to greenhouse gas emissions and the production of particulates. Solar panels are expensive and the level of sunlight is not constant, so output can vary. Wind turbines, on the other hand, require low maintenance and emit no greenhouse gases or particulates. There may be some days without wind but not enough for the disadvantages to outweigh the advantages.

13. **Lines should be drawn from** Solar **to** It is ideal if the panels face south; **from** Hydroelectric **to** A dam needs to be built across a river **and from** Wind **to** Build in exposed areas.
    [1 for each correct line up to a maximum of 2.]

14. (a) Fossil fuels (e.g. coal):
    Any advantage from: Convenient to use; Easy to transport; Power stations can be built anywhere; High energy output
    Any disadvantage from: Emission of carbon dioxide; Emission of sulfur dioxide; Emission of particulates; Contributes to global warming/climate change; Non-renewable
    Nuclear fuel:
    Any advantage from: Convenient to use; Easy to transport; High energy output; No emission of greenhouse gases; No emission of particulates; Reliable energy source
    Any disadvantage from: Nuclear waste difficult to dispose of; Radioactivity from the fuel rods and spent fuel; Perceived threat to the public; Power stations need a water supply.
    (b) (i) Wind turbines have a low power output, so you need a lot of wind turbines to match the output of a conventional power station; It is not always windy, so power output is not reliable.
    (ii) **Any two advantages from:** Out of sight so little visual pollution; Windy locations; No buildings or hills to cause turbulence
    Any two disadvantages from: Expensive to build; Inaccessible for repair; Long cables needed to transport electricity inland; Danger to shipping
    (iii) **Any two from:** Hydroelectric; Wave; Tidal

15. (a) Solar energy:
    Any one from: The intensity of light from the Sun varies and so the output from the solar panels will also vary; The intensity of sunlight in the UK is never large. This means that solar will not be able to supply the required quantity of electrical energy.
    Wind power: It is not always windy so some days will give little energy output.
    (b) The cost and supply of gas is controlled by other countries. This means that the UK's energy supply could be affected by world affairs.
    (c) **This is a model answer which would score full marks:**
    Alternative energy is a developing area but cannot provide all of the energy that the UK needs at the moment, although it can make a significant contribution. Solar and wind sources are unreliable and their output of energy is small compared to the needs of the National Grid. Hydroelectric power stations are expensive to build and there are only a few suitable sites for them. This means that fossil fuels and nuclear power must provide the bulk of our energy needs. The UK has coal, so has control of that energy source as it does with wind and hydroelectric. Nuclear fuels come from stable areas of the world, but some of the gas and oil needed does not and they are expensive to import. It makes sense not to rely on one source.

16. (a) Rate = Energy in ÷ Time in seconds
    = 10 000 ÷ 25 = 400(J/s or W)
    [1 for correct working but wrong answer]
    (b) (i) Current = Power rating ÷ Voltage
    = 1150 ÷ 230 = 5 (amps)
    [1 for correct working but wrong answer]

(ii) Energy transferred = Power rating × Time in seconds
= 1150 × 3 × 60 = 207 000 (joules)
[1 for correct working but wrong answer]
(iii) Units used = Power rating in kW × Time in hours
= 1.150 × (3 ÷ 60) = 0.0575(kWh)
[1 for correct working but wrong answer]
(iv) Total cost = Units used × Cost per unit
= 0.0575 × 8 = 0.46p
[1 for correct working but wrong answer]
(c) (i) Useful power output = (Percentage efficiency ÷ 100) × Power rating in watts
= (65 ÷ 100) × 2000 = 1300(W)
[1 for correct working but wrong answer]
(ii) Useful work done = Useful power out × Time in seconds = 1300 × 5 × 60 = 390 000 (joules)
[1 for correct working but wrong answer]

Module P4: Explaining Motion
(Pages 35–46)

1. (a) (i) Samantha ran 150m in 20 seconds **should be ticked**.
   (ii) Speed = Distance ÷ Time = 1200 ÷ 150 = 8(m/s)
   [1 for correct working but wrong answer]
   (iii) The runner is unlikely to run at exactly the same speed for the whole race.
   (iv) The speed (of an object) at a particular time
   (b) Velocity includes direction.
   (c) **Any one from:** Acceleration is the rate at which the velocity of an object changes; Acceleration is a measure of how quickly an object speeds up or slows down.

2. gradient; speed; faster **and** horizontal **should be ringed**.

3. (a) False
   (b) True
   (c) True
   (d) False

4. (a) [graph: horizontal line at 5m]
   [1 for horizontal line at 5m]
   (b) [graph: sloping line with gradient of 5]
   [1 for sloping line with a gradient of 5]

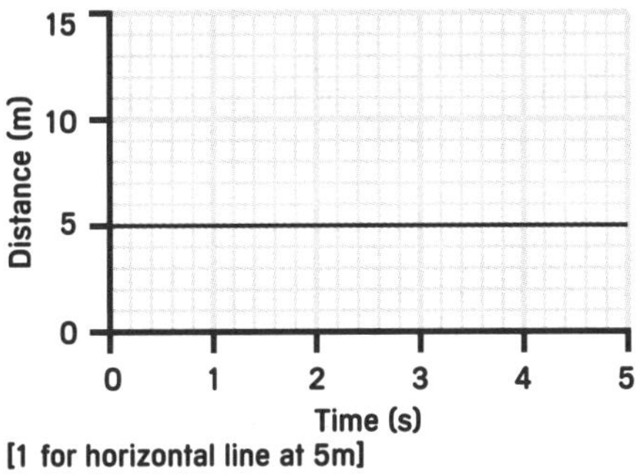

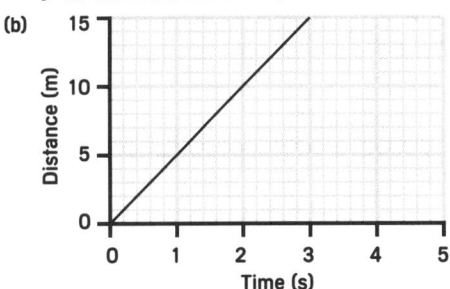

5. (a) gradient; acceleration; quickly **and** horizontal **should be ringed**.
   (b) (i) Point A marked at (0, 0)
   (ii) Point B marked anywhere on line between (3, 15) and (5, 15)
   (iii) Point C marked anywhere on line between (0, 0) and (3, 15)

6. (a) **Any one from:** Change in velocity and Time taken for change; Force and Mass
   (b) metres per second^2 (m/s^2) **should be ticked**.

(c) (i) Acceleration = Change in velocity ÷ Time
= 15 ÷ 5 = 3 m/s^2
[1 for correct working but wrong answer]
(ii) Acceleration = Change in velocity ÷ Time
= 14 ÷ 4 = 3.5 m/s^2
[1 for correct working but wrong answer]
(iii) Deceleration = Change in velocity ÷ Time
= 40 ÷ 2 = 20 m/s^2
[1 for correct working but wrong answer]

7. (a) [speed-time graph]
[1 for correctly labelling the x-axis, including units; 1 for correctly labelling the y-axis, including units; 1 for correctly plotting the points]
(b) (i) Acceleration = 10 ÷ 4 = 2.5(m/s^2)
[1 for correct working but wrong answer]
(ii) Acceleration = 4 ÷ 4 = 1(m/s^2)
[1 for correct working but wrong answer]
(c) Average speed = Total distance ÷ Total time
= 228 ÷ 20 = 11.4(m/s)
[1 for correct working but wrong answer]

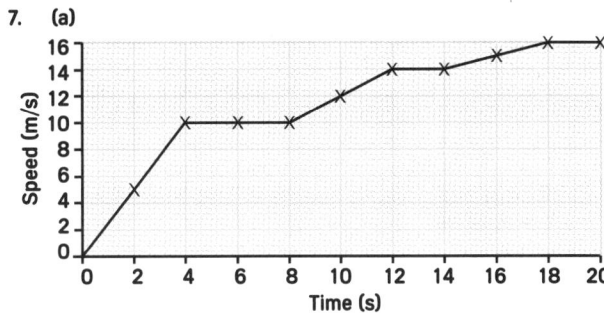

8. (a)

Name of Force	Description of Force
Friction	Acts to slow things down when two surfaces rub against each other
Air resistance	**Friction caused by objects moving through air**
Reaction of the surface	Pushes up on the bottom of a cup sitting on a table and stops the cup sinking into the table
Gravity	**Any one from: Attracts two masses towards each other; Attracts a mass towards the centre of the Earth**

(b) **This is a model answer which would score full marks:**
A jet engine pushes gas backwards (action), forcing the jet forwards (reaction). Initially the forwards force is greater than the air resistance, so the jet accelerates. As the speed increases, so does the air resistance until the air resistance balances the forwards force. When the forces are balanced the jet will continue forward at a steady speed until a braking force is applied to slow it down.
(c) **Any two suitable examples with suitable explanation, e.g.** The brakes of a car **[1]** use friction between the wheels and the pads to slow down the car **[1]**; When climbing a wall **[1]**, friction between hands and feet and the wall provides grip **[1]**.

9. (a) The size of the force **and** The direction of the force **should be ticked**.
(b) The combined effect of all the forces acting on an object **[1]**, resulting from adding the forces together **[1]**.
(c) (i) → 3000N **[1]**; The car will accelerate / speed up **[1]**.
(ii) ← 2000N **[1]**; The car will decelerate / slow down **[1]**.
(iii) 0N **[1]**; The car will continue at the same velocity **[1]**.
(d) (i) 2N **[1]** to the right **[1]**
(ii) 3N **[1]** up **[1]**
(e) (i) Noah
(ii) Anna
(iii) Bob

10. (a) | B | A | D | C |

[1 for each correctly placed up to a maximum of 3.]
(b) **This is a model answer which would score full marks:**
As Caitlin exits the plane, the only force acting on her is gravity, so she accelerates downwards. As her speed increases, so does the air resistance, so her acceleration decreases. When the air resistance, equals the force of gravity, the forces are balanced and she falls at a constant speed. When Caitlin's parachute opens, air resistance increases and is then greater than the force of gravity, so she decelerates. As her speed reduces, so does the air resistance until the two forces become balanced. She then falls at a lower constant speed than previously until she hits the ground and becomes stationary.

11. (a) A lorry travelling at 50mph **should be ticked**.
    (b) not change; mass; velocity ['mass' and 'velocity' in any order]

12.
Momentum (kg m/s)	Mass (kg)	Velocity (m/s)
500	50	10
30 000	1000	30
3000	**100**	30
800	400	**2**

13. **This is a model answer which would score full marks:**
The crumple zone of a car is designed to increase the time of the collision. This reduces the momentum over a longer period of time, which reduces the acceleration. As a result the force exerted on the people in the car is reduced. This results in fewer injuries.

14. (a) Use the tape measure to measure a set distance [1] and the stopwatch to measure the time taken to travel this distance, so that its velocity can be calculated [1]. Use the electronic balance to measure the mass of the trolley [1].
    (b) (i) At 2m/s, 1J [1]; At 4m/s, 4J [1]
    (ii) As the velocity increases, the kinetic energy increases [1]. As the velocity doubles, the kinetic energy more than doubles [1].
    (iii) The graph should be extended to pass through the origin [1]. At zero velocity, there is no kinetic energy [1].

15. (a) (i) A pendulum at the top of its swing **should be ticked**.
    (ii) A cyclist at the top of a hill **should be ticked**.
    (b) gravitational; kinetic
    (c) Gravitational potential energy
    = Weight × Vertical height difference
    = 500 × 100 = 50 000J
    [1 for correct working; 1 for correct answer; 1 for correct units]

16. Work done = Force × Distance moved in the direction of the force
    Work done = 10 × 500 = 5000J
    [1 for correct working; 1 for correct answer; 1 for correct units]

17. (a) Average velocity = Total displacement ÷ Total time
    = 0 ÷ 12 = 0(m/s)
    [1 for correct working but wrong answer]
    (b) Average speed = Total distance ÷ Total time
    = (12 + 12) ÷ 12 = 24 ÷ 12 = 2(m/s)
    [1 for correct working but wrong answer]
    (c) Speed = Distance ÷ Time = 12 ÷ 6 = 2(m/s)
    [1 for correct working but wrong answer]
    (d) **Any one from:** The object is not moving at a constant speed; The object is accelerating or decelerating.

18. (a) changing; speeding up; slowing down
    (b) Average speed = Total distance ÷ Total time
    = 200 ÷ 25 = 8(m/s)
    [1 for correct working but wrong answer]

19. **This is a model answer which would score full marks:**
The velocity of the car increases between A and B as the car accelerates from rest. The velocity decreases between B and C and the car comes to rest momentarily before the velocity then increases between C and D but with the car travelling in the opposite direction. The velocity decreases again between D and E until the car comes to rest.

20. (a) [graph showing distance (m) vs time (s), straight line from (0,0) to (20,100) then curved line levelling off at (30,130)]

[1 for straight line from (0, 0) to (20, 100); 1 for curved line from (20, 100) levelling off at (30, 130)]
(b) 110(m)
(c) Kinetic energy = $\frac{1}{2}$ × Mass × Velocity^2
560 = $\frac{1}{2}$ × 70 × Velocity^2
Velocity^2 = 16
Velocity = 4m/s
[1 for correct working; 1 for correct answer; 1 for correct units]

Module P5: Electric Circuits
(Pages 47–58)

1. current; voltage; proportional; voltage; doubled

2. (a) The rod has lost electrons **should be ticked**.
    (b) There are free electrons in the wire to allow a current to flow; A current will flow in the wire **and** Some energy in the wire will be lost as heat on discharge **should be ticked**.
    (c) The two rods will repel.

3. (a) (i) $V_1 = V_2 + V_3$
    $20 = V_2 + 8$
    $V_2 = 12$ (volts)
    [1 for correct working but wrong answer]
    (ii) V = IR
    12 = 2 × R
    R = 6(Ω)
    [1 for correct working but wrong answer]
    (b) (i) $V_2 = 20 - 4 = 16(V)$
    V = IR
    16 = I × 16
    I = 1 (amp)
    [1 for correct working but wrong answer]
    (ii) Work done = Voltage × Units of charge moved
    = 16 × 3 = 48 (joules)
    [1 for correct working but wrong answer]
    (c) **This is a model answer which would score full marks:**
    The resistance of the thermistor rises as it cools in the ice. The value shown by V_3 would increase and the value shown on V_2 would decrease. The value of the current in the circuit would decrease as the total resistance increases.

4. charge; amps; conductors; not used

5. Wires contain electrons [1]. The battery pushes these electrons around the complete circuit [1]. Energy is carried from the battery and lost as heat in the resistor [1]. Collisions occur between the moving electrons and vibrating ions, generating heat in the resistor [1].

6. (a) Jason
   (b) Toni

7. (a) There will be no force on the wire **should be ticked**.
   (b) **Any two from:** Move the magnet away from the coil; Reverse the magnet and move it towards the coil; Rotate the coil through 180° and move the magnet towards it.
   (c) A and C **should be ticked**.

8. (a) (i) Current = Power rating in watts ÷ Voltage
          = (1.84 × 1000) ÷ 230 = 8(A)
          [1 for correct working but wrong answer]
       (ii) Voltage = Current × Resistance
           so Resistance = Voltage ÷ Current
           Resistance = 230 ÷ 8 = 28.75(Ω)
           [1 for correct working but wrong answer]
   (b) (i) For each lamp Voltage = Current × Resistance
          so Current = Voltage ÷ Resistance
          Current = 230 ÷ 460 = 0.5(A)
          So the total current from the mains = 3 × 0.5 = 1.5(A)
          [1 for correct working but wrong answer]
       (ii) Current = Voltage ÷ Resistance
           = 230 ÷ (460 + 460 + 460) = 0.17(A)
           [1 for correct working but wrong answer]

9. **This is a model answer which would score full marks:**

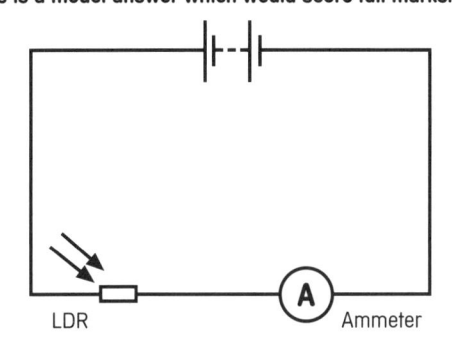

   Lam should place the torch bulb a short distance from the light dependent resistor (LDR) and measure the distance with a ruler. He should then measure the current reading on the ammeter and record both in a table. He should repeat this process for at least six different distances, which should be repeated and averaged. Lam could then plot a graph of current against distance to show the relationship.

10. (a) (i)

Distance of the Torch from the Component (cm)	Voltage (V)	Current (A)	Resistance (Ω)
20	6	0.6	10
40	6	0.5	12
60	6	**0.4**	15
80	6	0.3	**20**
100	6	0.2	30

   (ii) Light dependent resistor (LDR)
   (b) Yes **[1]**. As the distance increases from 20cm to 40cm, the current reduces by 0.1A. However, when it increases from 40cm to 80cm the current reduces by 0.2A **[1]**.
   (c) Toni **[1]** because with more readings over a larger range it will become clear if there is a trend. This will give more support to her conclusion **[1]**.

11. A_1: 0.4(A);
    A_3: 0.4(A);
    V_2: 3(V);
    V_3: 3(V)

12. (a) (i) The component heats up.
        (ii) The resistance of short wires is very small when compared to the resistance of components in the circuit (so it can be ignored in calculations).
    (b) The greater the voltage across a component, the greater the current flowing through it **and** Two insulators with similar charges will repel each other **should be ticked**.
    (c) A direct current from a battery is a current that flows in the same direction all the time, whereas the alternating current from the mains is a current that reverses direction many times a second.

13. A transformer can change the size of a direct current (d.c.) **should be ticked**.

14. (a) Increase the voltage of the battery (or the current from it); Use more turns of wire on the coil; Use a stronger magnet in the motor.
    (b) A commutator ensures that the direction of the current is reversed **[1]** at an appropriate point in each revolution **[1]**.

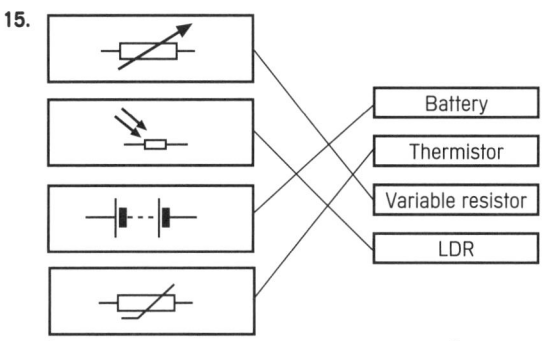

15. [1 for each correct line up to a maximum of 3.]

16. (a) As the magnet rotates, magnetic field lines cut the wire, generating a voltage (potential difference) across the coil.
    (b) **This is a model answer which would score full marks:**
        As the magnet rotates, the direction of the voltage (potential difference) changes every half turn of the magnet. The value of the voltage also changes every half turn and is at a maximum when the poles of the magnet are parallel to the coil with the most field lines cutting the wire in the coil.

17. C and D **should be ticked**.

18. A change in the resistance of one component in the circuit will not affect the potential differences across the other components **should be ticked**.

19. (a) Units used = 768 ÷ 8 = 96(kWh)
        [1 for correct working but wrong answer]
    (b) Units used in kWh = Power rating in kW × Time in hours
        So Power rating = Units used ÷ Time in hours
        = 96 ÷ (2 × 24) = 2(kW)
        [1 for correct working but wrong answer]
    (c) Units used = 40 ÷ 8 = 5
        Units used in kWh = Power rating in kW × Time in hours
        So Time in hours = Units used ÷ Power rating in kW
        = 5 ÷ 0.25 = 20 (hours)
        [1 for correct working but wrong answer]

20. | E | C | B | A | D |

    [1 for each correctly placed up to a maximum of 4.]
    [If there is an incorrect answer then C before B gains 1 mark; A before D gains 1 mark. Any two letters in the correct order gains 1 mark.]

21. (a) **This is a model answer which would score full marks:**
    The alternating current flowing due to the 230V alternating voltage induces a changing magnetic field in the primary coil. This flows backwards and forwards around the soft iron core as iron is easily magnetised and demagnetised. The changing magnetic field in the soft iron core passes through the secondary coil, inducing an alternating voltage (potential difference) across it. As the ratio of turns in the primary coil to the secondary coil is 100:1, the voltage is stepped down to 2.3V.

    (b) $\dfrac{\text{Primary voltage}}{\text{Secondary voltage}} = \dfrac{\text{No of turns on the primary coil}}{\text{No of turns on secondary coil}}$
    Primary voltage = (40 ÷ 320) × 160 = 20(V)
    [1 for correct working but wrong answer]

Module P6: Radioactive Materials
(Pages 59–69)

1. C and E **should be ticked**.

2. **Lines should be drawn from** Alpha **to** Stopped by paper; **from** Beta **to** Stopped by 4mm of aluminium but not by paper; **and from** Gamma **to** Only stopped by several centimetres of lead.
   [1 for each correct line up to a maximum of 2.]

3. A microwave oven **should be ticked**.

4. (a) (i) Peer review. Nine different countries and 7000 individual cases were used to produce the study.
    (ii) Radon gas emits short-range alpha particles which cannot penetrate the outside layer of the skin **[1]**. Only when it enters the lungs can it cause serious damage to body cells **[1]**.
   (b) **This is a model answer which would score full marks:**
    The report does not look at other possible causes, for example smoking or genetics (history of lung cancer in the family). In addition, the study does not look at variables such as age, sex or ethnic group. People can live in areas of high exposure to radon gas but still develop lung cancer for other reasons. Not all people exposed to radon gas develop lung cancer. The report does not mention if a control group was studied, possibly similar people in areas with very low radon gas emissions, to see if the reported cases of lung cancer were clearly lower.

5. There are only protons and neutrons in the nucleus of an atom **should be ticked**.

6. (a) (i) Gamma
    (ii) Beta
    (iii) Alpha
    (iv) Gamma
   (b) (i) **This is a model answer which would score full marks:**
    The teacher must use forceps to handle the sources and keep both himself and the students at a sensible distance from the sources at all times, to avoid too much irradiation. For each source in turn, place the paper in front of it and use the Geiger counter to measure the radiation passing through in a certain time. The Geiger counter should be only a few centimetres from the source and the counts for each source should be recorded. The time, measured with the stopwatch, and the distance of the source from the Geiger counter should be kept the same for all the measurements of radiation. Repeat the process for the sheet of aluminium and the piece of lead.
    (ii) Gamma radiation
    (iii) The background count (to subtract from his experimental readings)
   (c) (i) Ionising radiation can damage living cells/cause cancer/cause mutations **[1]** but background radiation is at a safe level **[1]**.
    (ii) Sievert
    (iii) Exposure to ionising radiation

7. (a) (i) The radiologist
    (ii) The patient
    (iii) Irradiation
   (b) The patient will be emitting beta particles due to the radioiodine and these can travel a short distance in the air **[1]**. By keeping a reasonable distance, the relatives will be out of range of the beta particles **[1]**.

8. (a) Gamma
   (b) **This is a model answer which would score full marks:**
    A source with a half-life of a few days should be chosen so that the radiation can fall to a safe level in a time long enough to destroy the tumour but not so long that it causes major damage to living cells. A source with a half-life of a few hours would decay before it could successfully irradiate the tumour, whilst a source with a half-life of a few weeks would be likely to cause damage to living tissue because they would be exposed to high levels of radiation for too long.

9. (a) (i) Y
    (ii) Z
    (iii) X
   (b) The time taken for the activity of a radioactive source to fall to half of its starting value is called the half-life; The further you are from a radioactive source, the less radiation your body is exposed to **and** Lead shields are used in hospitals to protect medical staff from exposure to radiation **should be ticked**.

10. half-life; alpha; beta

11. (a) (i) Too much exposure could lead to damage to the body cells or radiation sickness.
     (ii) **Any suitable answer, e.g.** A worker in the nuclear industry; Medical staff; Nuclear research scientist
    (b) (i) A controlled dose of intense ionising radiation can be administered to the affected area for a limited amount of time **[1]** by a tracer or by a beam of gamma rays to kill cancer cells **[1]**.
     (ii) The patient: There is a small risk of damaging cells around the cancer cells.
     The medical staff: There is a higher risk of damaging their own body cells / getting cancer due to increased exposure.
    (c) **Any two from:** Use a lead shield; Keep as large a distance as possible from the source; Limit the time of exposure to ionising radiation.

12. A and D **should be ticked**.

13. **Any four from:** Radon; Medical; Food; Cosmic rays; Gamma rays from rocks or buildings; Nuclear industry; Nuclear weapons testing / fallout

14. *v*: 234; *w*: 2; *x*: 234; *y*: −1

15. (a) (i) 1 minute **should be ticked**.
     (ii) 4 minutes **should be ringed**.
    (b) $208 \times \left(\frac{1}{2}\right)^5 = 6.5(g)$
    [1 for correct working but wrong answer]
    (c) The nucleus loses four protons **[1]** and four neutrons **[1]**.

16. (a) **This is a model answer which would score full marks:**
    A neutron is absorbed by the nucleus and it makes the nucleus unstable causing it to split into two almost equal parts, which become radioactive waste. Three neutrons are released and a large quantity of energy is released, mostly in the form of heat. In a nuclear reactor, one neutron, on average, goes on to further fission reactions with uranium nuclei, leading to large releases of energy and a small amount of radioactive waste material being produced.

(b) Each fission releases energy and further neutrons **[1]** and at least one neutron from each fission goes on to further fission, releasing more energy **[1]**.
(c) Control rods are raised or lowered to absorb fewer or more neutrons **[1]**, so that, on average, just one neutron from each fission goes on to further fission, meaning a constant rate of energy release **[1]**.

17. Isotopes of the same element always have the same number of protons **and** Isotopes of an element always have the same number of protons but a different number of neutrons **should be ticked**.

18. (a) **Any suitable answer, e.g.** The ionising radiation used is gamma as it passes through the body and there is only a small risk of damage to body cells **[1]**. It can be detected easily outside the body and used to produce detailed images of internal organs **[1]**. Medical staff will use sources with a short half-life so that they are quickly eliminated from the body **[1]**. They will keep the dosage as low as possible (ALARA principle) and monitor their exposure to radiation using special film badges **[1]**. **['Glass shields containing lead can be used to reduce exposure to gamma radiation' is also acceptable.]**
(b) An isotope of thorium, atomic number 90 **should be ticked**.

19. (a) There are two forces that are balanced **[1]**. The repulsive force between the positively charged protons trying to force the nucleus apart is balanced by the strong force which is an attractive, short-ranged force between the particles in the nucleus, and this holds it together **[1]**.
(b) (i) $E = mc^2 = (3.1 \times 10^{-28}) \times (9 \times 10^{16})$
   $= 2.79 \times 10^{-11}$ (J)
   [1 for correct working but wrong answer]
(ii) No. of nuclei $= 1.0J \div (2.79 \times 10^{-11} J)$
   $= 3.58 \times 10^{10}$
   [1 for correct working but wrong answer]

Module P7: Further Physics – Studying the Universe (Pages 70–96)

1. (a) 24 hours **should be ticked**.
(b) East to west **should be ticked**.

2. (a) The Earth orbits the Sun, so the position of the Earth in July is different from in January **[1]** and the Sun blocks the view of stars that could be seen in January **[1]**.
(b) The right ascension

3. Stars are stationary in the sky, **[1]** whilst the planets move in complicated patterns compared to the background of these stationary stars **[1]**.

4. (a) Just over 24 hours **should be ticked**.
(b) 28 days **should be ticked**.
(c) reflected; Moon; away from; towards
(d) As the Moon orbits the Earth, an observer on Earth can see different parts of the Moon at different times of the month **[1]**. The observer could see the half in darkness or the half in light, and all the points in between **[1]**.
(e) While the Earth has rotated once **[1]**, the Moon will have completed $\frac{1}{28}$ of an orbit **[1]**, so will be over a different part of the Earth's surface.

5. (a) New Moon **should be ticked**.
(b) A: 4; B: 3; C: 1; D: 2
   [1 for each correct up to a maximum of 3.]

6. (a) Refraction; Light slows down
(b) A converging lens
(c) **Any one from:** Inwards; Towards the principal axis
(d) less; long; more; short
   [1 for each correct up to a maximum of 3.]

(e) (i) Dioptre
(ii) Power = 1 ÷ Focal length in metres
   = 1 ÷ 0.5 = 2 dioptres
   [1 for correct working but wrong answer]
(f) The image is real **[1]** and the same size as the object **[1]**.

7. (a) (i) Eyepiece lens; Objective lens
(ii) Eyepiece lens
(b) They use a mirror instead of a lens for the objective **should be ticked**.
(c) **Any suitable diagram, e.g.**

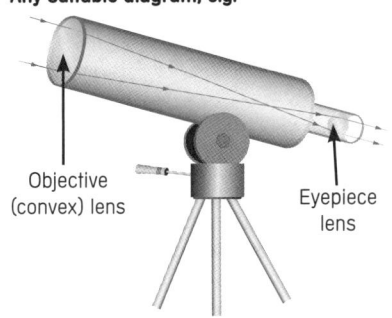

   [1 for each correctly labelled lens; 1 for correctly drawn rays]

8. (a) Using a mirror instead of a lens means that bigger telescopes which collect more light can be built **[1]** and, because they collect more light, this kind of telescope can view objects that are further away **[1]**.
(b) Eyepiece lens; Objective mirror

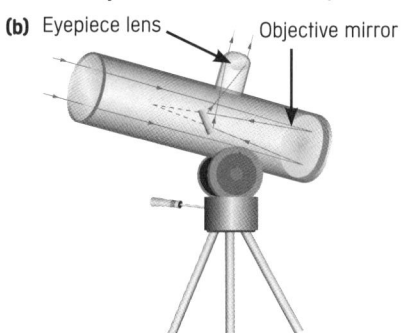

   [1 for each correct label]

9. (a) Reflection; Refraction; Diffraction
(b)

   [1 for showing wave changing direction; 1 for showing wave fronts closer together]

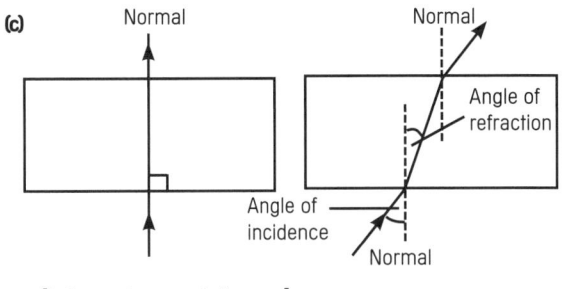

(c)

   [1 for each correct diagram]

10. This is a model answer which would score full marks:
When a light wave crosses a boundary between one medium and another the speed may change if the density of the medium is different. If the light approaches the boundary at an angle other than 90°, the light will change direction. If the light travels from a less dense medium to a denser one, for example, from air to glass, its speed decreases and it bends towards the normal. If it travels from a denser medium to a less dense one, for example, from glass to air, its speed increases and it is bent away from the normal. This is called refraction.

11. (a) They spread out from the edges.
(b) **Any one from:** The wave would not be diffracted; The wave would continue at the same speed and in the same direction.

12. This is a model answer which would score full marks:
When waves pass through a narrow gap or past an obstacle, they spread out. This is known as diffraction. When the radio waves go past the hill, the radio waves spread out around the hill and the radio signal can be picked up by the house. This happens to the radio waves because they have very long wavelengths and can be easily diffracted. Microwaves can also be diffracted but they need a much smaller gap or obstacle to pass through or around. This is because the wavelength of microwaves is very small. Therefore the microwaves are not diffracted around the hill and the microwaves from the transmitter do not reach the house.

13. (a) The parallax angle of a star is half the angle moved (in six months) **[1]** against a background of distant stars **[1]**.
(b) (i) False
(ii) False
(iii) False
(c) [Diagram showing parallax angle]

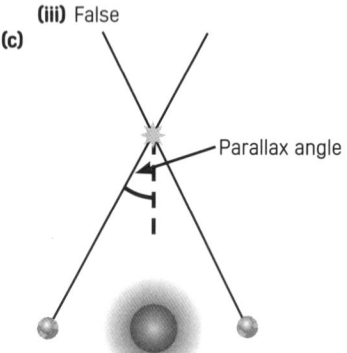

(d)
Star	Distance (pc)	Parallax angle (arcseconds)
Sirius	2.64	**0.38**
Arcturus	**22.7**	0.044
Barnard's Star	**1.82**	0.55
Proxima Centauri	1.30	**0.77**

14. (a) Distance in parsecs = 1 ÷ Parallax angle in arcseconds
Distance = 1 ÷ 0.5 = 2 (parsecs)
[1 for correct working but wrong answer]
(b) For distant galaxies the parallax angle is too small to be measured.
(c) (i) A star that pulses **[1]**. Its brightness changes on a regular basis **[1]**.
(ii) **This is a model answer which would score full marks:**
Cepheid variable stars pulse in brightness and their period is related to their luminosity. Fuzzy objects called spiral nebulae had been seen with telescopes and were thought to be part of our galaxy. Observations of Cepheid variable stars in spiral nebulae and calculations of the distance to them showed that spiral nebulae were in fact separate galaxies, not part of the Milky Way, and that the Universe was much larger than was originally thought.

15. (a) The amount of energy the star gives out
(b) Its size **and** Its temperature **should be ticked**.

16. Speed of recession in km/s
= Hubble constant in km/s per Mpc × Distance in Mpc
Speed of recession = 70 × 80 = 5600(km/s)
[1 for correct working but wrong answer]

17. (a) (i) If the volume is reduced, the molecules will have less distance to travel between the walls of the container **[1]**. Therefore there will be more collisions per second **[1]** and, as a result, a higher pressure **[1]**.
(ii) As the temperature rises, the molecules have a greater kinetic energy so they travel faster **[1]**. Therefore there will be a greater change in momentum during collisions **[1]**, leading to a greater force on the container **[1]** (and a greater pressure).
(b) (i) −273(°C)
(ii) At absolute zero the molecules would have no kinetic energy **[1]**. Therefore they would not be moving so there would be no volume **[1]**. There would also be no collisions with the walls of the container **[1]** and so pressure would be zero **[1]**.
(c)
Gas	Temperature (°C)	Temperature (K)
Oxygen	−20	**253**
Helium	**−153**	120
Water vapour	101	**374**

(d) (i) $T_1 = 20°C = 293K$; $T_2 = 200°C = 473K$
$P_2 \div T_2 = P_1 \div T_1$ so $P_2 = P_1 \times T_2 \div T_1$
$P_2 = 10^5 \times 473 \div 293 = 1.61 \times 10^5 (Pa)$
[1 for correct working but wrong answer]
(ii) The volume would have been halved.

18. (a) (i) Gravity
(ii) Hydrogen
(iii) The temperature will rise.
(b) (i) (Nuclear) fusion
(ii) hydrogen; helium; energy
(c) (i) The protostar only gives out a continuous spectra covering radio and near infrared but the Sun has a continuous spectra across all parts of the electromagnetic spectrum.
(ii) Nuclear fusion has been going on in the Sun for millions of years, so it will have helium spectral lines that are visible **[1]**. The surface temperature of the protostar is too cool to give out a full spectra because fusion has not yet begun **[1]**.

19. (a) Large lenses are heavy and can distort under their own weight, making the image unclear.
(b) By then there was too much light pollution (in Greenwich)
(c) **Any four from:** Less light pollution; High elevation so less atmosphere for the light to pass through; Frequent cloudless nights; Low atmospheric pollution; Dry air
(d) **Any three from:** Cost of building and setting up; Finding a suitable location; Creating access to the telescope; Working conditions for employees; Power supply; Environmental and social issues

20. By using visual methods to observe and record data; By using a computer to locate and process images

21. The cost must be considered when building an observatory **and** Telescopes with large mirrors are used to capture more light **should be ticked**.

22. X is a supergiant, Y is a white dwarf and Z is a red giant; The Sun would be approximately placed near the middle of the main sequence **and** The luminosity of a star decreases as it passes through the main sequence **should be ticked**.

23. (a) **Any two from:** There are mainly clear night skies; There is low atmospheric pollution; The site is at a high elevation (so there is less atmosphere that the light from stars has to travel through); The site is far from built-up areas so there is less light pollution.
    (b) **Any two from:** Cost; Working conditions for employees; Environmental and social impact near the observatory; Availability of electricity supplies
    (c) There is a limit to the size of lens that can be used due to the weight of glass causing distortion and therefore poor image quality **[1]**. Unlike a lens, a mirror can be supported underneath, so can be made much larger **[1]**.
    (d) To produce a more detailed image; To reduce the effect of diffraction
    (e) **Any two from:** Few clear nights for observing; More atmospheric instability; More light pollution; Environmental issues connected with building in a national park

24. (a) Alice; Mel **[Both needed for 1 mark.]**
    (b) luminosity; temperature **[these two in any order]**

25. (a) (i) Hydrogen; Helium
        (ii) Copper; Zinc
    (b) carbon; nitrogen; oxygen **[nitrogen and oxygen in any order]**
    (c) From supernovae
    (d) The core of a red giant has much more mass in a given space so has a greater density than the Sun **[1]**. This results in nuclei being packed closer together **[1]**, which makes fusion much more likely as there is a much greater chance of successful collisions between the nuclei than in the core of the Sun **[1]**.

26. (a) (i) The core of Aldebaran would be hotter than the core of the Sun.
        (ii) There is more pressure in the core of a red giant than in the core of a main sequence star **[1]**. This is due to the core of the red giant collapsing as the outer layers expand **[1]**. Therefore the rate of nuclear fusion is greater in the core of Aldebaran than in the core of the Sun **[1]** and this generates more heat.
    (b) Convection; Radiation of photons

27. (a) (i) **Lines should be drawn from** Hubble telescope **to** Can be damaged by solar flares; **from** Jodrell Bank radio telescope **to** Affected most by diffraction; **and from** Newtonian reflector **to** Images distorted by an unstable atmosphere.
        [1 for each correct line up to a maximum of 2.]
        (ii) **This is a model answer which would score full marks:**
        The atmosphere is an absorber of all wavelengths of the electromagnetic spectrum other than the visual region, microwaves and some radio waves. This limits the types of telescope that can be used on the Earth's surface. There are other problems to consider as well. The air refracts visual light, affecting the quality of the image, and air currents caused by localised heating effects can make images of distant objects seem unstable. Also, water vapour in clouds can block visible light and absorb radio waves close to the microwave region.
    (b) (i) Exoplanets
        (ii) Unexplained variations in the star's brightness; Wobble of the star on its axis
        (iii) No light from the distant object was absorbed by the atmosphere **[1]**, giving the Hubble telescope a more detailed image **[1]**.
        (iv) The behaviour of other planetary systems provides evidence of how our solar system formed **[1]** and what might happen to it in the future **[1]**.

28. (a) (i) 3127°C
        (ii) Spica **should be ringed**.
        (iii) Antares **should be ringed**.
    (b) (i) It consists mainly of iron.
        (ii) Nuclei of elements heavier than iron

29. A, C and E **should be ticked**.

30. (a) (i) **Any two suitable explanations, e.g.** It is hard to detect signals coming in from all the possible directions at the same time; The signals will be very weak and might hardly register; There may be signals in different regions of the electromagnetic spectrum to the ones the detector is tuned to.
        (ii) **Any sensible argument supporting the fact that 'no signal has been received' is not proof that intelligent life does not exist, e.g.** Signals travel at the speed of light. They also spread out and weaken. It could be that the source is so far away that the signals have not yet reached Earth **[1]**. Also, they could be so weak that detection against background noise is too difficult **[1]**.
    (b) The telescope is set up to detect radio waves unlike Hubble **[1]** and radio waves pass through the Earth's atmosphere without being affected by absorption **[1]**.
    (c) As radio waves have a much larger wavelength than visible light **[1]** they suffer much more from diffraction when received by a telescope **[1]**.

31. (a) **This is a model answer which would score full marks:**
    One advantage of operating a telescope outside the Earth's atmosphere is that it avoids refraction effects on the light received, leading to clearer and more detailed images. Another advantage is that there is no atmosphere to absorb some of the light and no problems with heat from the Earth causing the atmosphere to become turbulent, which may distort the images obtained. However, operating a telescope outside the Earth's atmosphere would be expensive to set up and is difficult to access for repair and maintenance, which is a major disadvantage. Another disadvantage is that there is a strong chance of impacts outside the protection of the Earth's atmosphere and there is uncertainty about future space programmes to maintain it.
    (b) (i) **Any two from:** The cost of building and maintaining the telescope is shared; Expertise is shared
        (ii) Directly at the site of the telescope; Through the Internet; Through remote computer control
    (c) **Any three from:** Cost; Working conditions for employees; Environmental and social issues near the observatory; Availability of electricity supplies
    (d) (i) **Any three from:** Optical (refractor or reflector); X-ray; Gamma ray telescope; Radio telescope; Infrared telescope; Ultraviolet telescope
        (ii) Only a few wavelengths (ultraviolet, visible light, microwaves and radio waves) can get through the atmosphere without being seriously affected **[1]**. Therefore telescopes detecting waves from other regions of the electromagnetic spectrum would need to be used above the atmosphere **[1]**.

32. (a) Main sequence stars; Red giants; White dwarfs; Supergiants; Neutron stars (pulsars); Protostars; Red supergiants; Black holes **[Any three for 2 marks; any two for 1 mark.]**
    (b) **This is a model answer which would score full marks:**
    Each element, when given energy, can produce its own set of coloured emission lines in its spectrum. That element will also absorb wavelengths corresponding to those spectral lines from a continuous spectrum. By examining the absorption spectra from a star, these can be used to calculate the wavelengths of the absorption lines and then matched to the absorption spectra of different elements. The elements in the star can then be identified.
    (c) Astronomers share information so that they can use peer review to ensure the accuracy of any data published.

33. (a) A close star **should be ringed.**
   (b) Gravitational effects, e.g. wobble caused by a large mass very close to a star; Transient methods, e.g. the brightness of a star might be affected by the planet passing in front of it.
   (c) Any one from: An exoplanet would reflect very little light (photons) in the Earth's direction so would be hard to locate without a large telescope; A large mirror is needed to capture so few photons of light from an exoplanet in order to produce an image; Larger telescopes have better resolution so more detail can be observed.

34. Any three from: Computers can store the coordinates of every known star, galaxy or other astronomical object of interest, along with names and star types; Computer-stored data means a telescope can locate any star quickly; Computers can move the telescope with the rotation of the Earth to keep a continuous focus on any item of interest; Computers can store data and relay it to other computers anywhere in the world; Computers can filter out unwanted data in images and add false colour to images to enhance certain features.

35. (a) (i) At the red supergiant phase
   (ii) A massive explosion
   (iii) A neutron star; A black hole
   (b) (i) It will expand **[1]** and become a red giant **[1]**.
   (ii) A white dwarf **should be ticked.**
   (c) Any one from: Mass; Size

36. positive; negative; equator

37. (a) (i) Evelyn; Cindy **[Both needed for 1 mark.]**
   (ii) Ciara
   (b) (i) Apparent brightness; Luminosity over a period of time
   (ii) How far away the Cepheid variable is from Earth.

(c) They can calculate the distance of each Cepheid variable from Earth **[1]** and its corresponding value of the speed of recession from the red shift **[1]**. From the ratio of the speed of recession to the distance, the Hubble constant can be calculated **[1]**.

38. (a) (Heber) Curtis; (Harlow) Shapley
   (b) Spiral nebulae
   (c) This is a model answer which would score full marks: Harlow Shapley used his telescope to observe and measure the distances of a number of nebulae. He concluded that each nebula was a cluster of stars (globular cluster), which formed a sphere around the centre of our galaxy, the Milky Way. He also thought that the Milky Way was the complete Universe, which was challenged by Heber Curtis, leading to the Great Debate. Curtis had been studying 'spiral nebulae' and felt that these objects were very distant from the Milky Way. He thought that they were a similar size to the Milky Way and were galaxies.
   (d) Cepheid variables in one nebula
   (e) It is expanding **should be ticked**.

39. (a) The volume increases by a factor of 2^3 **[1]** = 8 **[1]**, so the pressure must decrease by a factor of 8 **[1]**.
   (b) $x = 3$; $y = 13$; $z = 6$
   (c) Any suitable answer, e.g. Electrons existing in certain energy levels of an atom can absorb an amount of energy (photons) **[1]** and move to higher energy levels **[1]**. So certain wavelengths corresponding to these movements will be subtracted from the whole spectrum, leaving dark lines in those positions **[1]**.

Electric Circuits — P5

(a) Which of the statements below is correct? Put a tick (✓) in the box next to the correct statement. [1]

Increasing the current will increase the force on the wire. ☐

Reversing the current will produce a force in the opposite direction. ☐

Increasing the strength of the magnetic field will increase the size of the force on the wire. ☐

There will be no force on the wire. ☐

(b) When a magnet is moved into a coil of wire connected to an ammeter, it indicates that a current is flowing. Describe **two** ways to produce a current in the opposite direction. [2]

1. _____

2. _____

(c) Electricity can be produced by rotating a magnet inside a coil of wire. An induced voltage will be produced across the coil. Below are some statements about possible changes that can be made.

  A Using a larger number of turns on the coil

  B Turning the magnet slowly and steadily

  C Using a stronger magnet

  D Turning the magnet around before allowing it to rotate

Which combination of changes will result in an **increased** induced voltage? Put a tick (✓) in the box next to the correct answer. [1]

A and C ☐

A and D ☐

B and C ☐

Another combination ☐

8. This question is about using the mains supply to power electrical devices.

  (a) A 1.84kW electric fire runs off the 230V mains.

    (i) What current does it take? [2]

_____ A

    (ii) What is the resistance of the fire? [2]

_____ Ω

P5 Electric Circuits

(b) Three bulbs, each with a resistance of 460Ω, are connected in parallel across the 230V mains.

(i) What is the current that the mains must provide in order to light all the lamps normally? [2]

.... A

(ii) If the bulbs were now arranged in series and light up, they will be dimmer. What current will flow through them? [2]

.... A

9. Lam is a student. He wants to demonstrate how the resistance of an LDR (light dependent resistor) depends on the brightness of a lamp. He has been given a battery, an LDR, some connecting leads, an ammeter and a working high-powered torch.

Describe an experiment that Lam could do to show how the resistance of an LDR varies with the brightness of the light. You could start by drawing a circuit diagram and explaining what readings need to be taken and how they are going to be recorded.

✎ *The quality of written communication will be assessed in your answer to this question.* [6]

Electric Circuits P5

10. Chloe has been given a component which has been placed in a box with a connecting wire attached to each end and a small hole in the box just above the component. The component, which also had a voltmeter connected in parallel with it, was then placed in a series circuit with a battery and an ammeter. By moving a torch close to the hole in the box above the component, she recorded the following readings:

Distance of the Torch from Component (cm)	Voltage (V)	Current (A)	Resistance (Ω)
20	6	0.6	10
40	6	0.5	12
60	6		15
80	6	0.3	
100	6	0.2	30

(a) (i) Complete the table by filling in the missing values for current and resistance. [2]

(ii) What component was most likely to be in the box? [1]

(b) Chloe thinks that there is a negative correlation between the current and the distance the torch is from the component. Do her results support this conclusion? Explain your answer. [2]

(c) Chloe wants to have more confidence in her conclusion and asks four friends how to improve the experiment.

Charlie: Repeat the readings lots of times.

Jo-Shun: Repeat the experiment using a higher voltage.

Toni: Repeat the experiment using a larger range of distances.

Faye: Draw a graph to see if there are any outliers.

Who gives the best advice? Explain your answer. [2]

P5 Electric Circuits

11. The diagram shows a series circuit where a battery lights two identical bulbs. Also connected in the circuit are three ammeters, A_1, A_2 and A_3, and three voltmeters, V_1, V_2 and V_3. The values of one ammeter and one voltmeter are shown. What are the values of the others? [4]

A_1: .... A

A_3: .... A

V_2: V

V_3: V

12. This question is about components in an electrical circuit.

(a) (i) Describe what happens to a component when a current passes through it. [1]

....

(ii) All components in a circuit have resistance. Why can the resistance of wires be ignored when doing calculations on small circuits? [1]

....

....

(b) Some students made the following statements. Which of them are true? Put ticks (✓) in the boxes next to the **two** correct statements. [2]

The greater the voltage across a component, the greater the current flowing through it. ☐

A component with 6V across it and having a resistance of 4Ω will have a current of 2A through it. ☐

In an insulator, there are lots of charges free to move. ☐

Two insulators with similar charges will repel each other. ☐

(c) Describe the difference between a direct current (d.c.) from a battery and an alternating current (a.c.) from the mains. [1]

....

....

Electric Circuits P5

13. Which of the following statements is **not** true? Put a tick (✓) in the box next to the **incorrect** statement. [1]

The voltage of the mains supply is 230V. ☐

A transformer can change the size of a direct current (d.c.). ☐

Mains electricity is produced by generators. ☐

Generators produce a voltage by electromagnetic induction. ☐

14. (a) You have been given an electric motor which is running as it is connected to a battery. What **three** changes could you make to the system in order to make your motor run faster? [3]

1. _____

2. _____

3. _____

(b) Explain why an electric motor has a commutator. [2]

_____

_____

_____

15. The symbols below are for components that are found in an electric circuit. Draw straight lines from the symbols to the correct names. [3]

Symbol	Name
(variable resistor symbol)	Battery
(LDR symbol)	Thermistor
(battery symbol)	Variable resistor
(thermistor symbol)	LDR

[Total: _____ / 77]

P5 Electric Circuits

Higher Tier

16. This question is about an a.c. generator.

   (a) Why is a voltage induced across a coil of wire by the rotation of a magnet near to it? [1]

   (b) Describe how the size of the induced voltage across the coil of the generator changes and how its direction changes during each rotation of the magnet.

   ✏ *The quality of written communication will be assessed in your answer to this question.* [6]

17. A thermistor is connected in series with a red lamp to form one branch of a circuit. An LDR is connected in series with a blue lamp to form another branch of the circuit. Both branches are now connected in parallel across a battery.

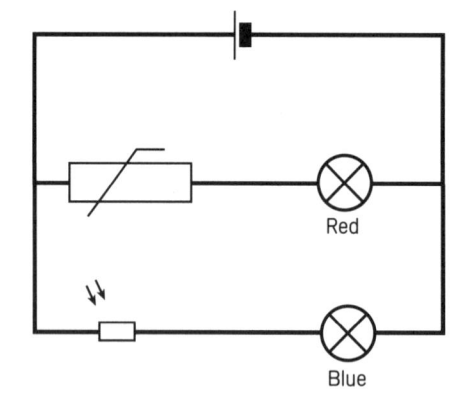

Below are some statements.

   A If the room heats up, the blue lamp will come on.

   B To get the red lamp on, I have to switch off the light in the room.

   C If it is hot in the room and I increase the brightness of the room, both the red and the blue lights come on.

D If the room gets colder and brighter, only the blue light comes on.

E If the blue light is on and I put the thermistor in ice, the blue light goes off.

Which of the statements are true? Put a tick (✓) in the box next to the combination of statements that is correct. [1]

A and D ☐   C, D and E ☐

B and D ☐   C and D ☐

A, B and E ☐

18. Which of the following statements is **not** true about a series circuit? Put a tick (✓) in the box next to the **incorrect** statement. [1]

The potential difference is largest across a large resistor, because more work is done by the charge moving through a large resistor than through a small one. ☐

A change in the resistance of one component in the circuit will not affect the potential differences across the other components. ☐

If a thermistor is connected in series with two fixed resistors, the potential difference across the fixed resistors will increase if the thermistor gets hot. ☐

The work done on each unit charge by the battery must equal the work done by it on the circuit components. ☐

19. This question is about how much energy appliances use.

Priscilla had a heater on for 2 days and it costs her 768p at a rate of 8p per kWh.

(a) How much energy did the heater use? [2]

_____ kWh

(b) What power rating was the heater? [2]

_____ kW

(c) She changed the heater and replaced it with a 250W heater. The cost of using this heater was 40p at the same rate of 8p per kWh. How long was the heater on for? [2]

_____ hours

P5 Electric Circuits

20. Below are some statements about how a transformer works. They are not in the correct order. Put the statements in the correct order by writing the letters in the empty boxes. [4]

A The alternating magnetic field keeps changing direction in the iron core inside the secondary coil.

B The alternating magnetic field changes direction in the iron core with the same frequency as the applied alternating voltage.

C The alternating current in the primary coil produces an alternating magnetic field.

D An alternating potential difference is induced in the secondary coil.

E An alternating voltage is applied to the primary coil.

Start | | | | | |

21. This question is about transformers.

(a) Explain how a step-down transformer, as used in a mobile phone charger, changes the 230V mains supply to 2.3V.

In your answer, you will need to consider how a voltage is induced in the secondary coil.

The quality of written communication will be assessed in your answer to this question. [6]

(b) A transformer has 40 turns on the primary coil and 320 turns on the secondary coil. If the output voltage is 160V, what is the voltage across the primary coil? [2]

_____ V

[Total: ____ / 27]

Radioactive Materials — P6

1. Rutherford, Geiger and Marsden carried out an alpha scattering experiment using gold. Below are some possible conclusions resulting from this experiment.

   A   The nucleus is very dense.
   B   An atom is mainly empty space.
   C   The nucleus is surrounded by negative electrons.
   D   The nucleus has a positive charge.
   E   Alpha particles must be negatively charged.
   F   The nucleus is very dense because it is not removed by alpha particles.

   Which of the statements were **not** conclusions resulting from this experiment? Put a tick (✓) in the box next to the correct combination of statements. [1]

   A and D ☐   A and F ☐   D and F ☐   C and E ☐   B and D ☐

2. Draw a straight line from each type of ionising radiation to the correct statement about its penetrating power. [2]

Radiation	Penetrating power
Alpha	Stopped by 4mm of aluminium but not by paper
Beta	Only stopped by several centimetres of lead
Gamma	Stopped by paper

3. Which one of the following items could not give off radiation that contributes to the background count measured by a Geiger counter? Put a tick (✓) in the box next to the correct answer. [1]

   A piece of granite rock ☐   A microwave oven ☐
   A piece of concrete ☐   A container of radon gas ☐

4. A report has been produced looking at the risk to health of radon gas. Exposure to radon is thought to increase the risk of developing lung cancer. Data from 13 studies carried out by scientists in nine European countries was used to produce the report. 7000 individual cases of lung cancer were studied and they showed a strong link between exposure to radon gas in the home and lung cancer.

   (a) (i) Why would scientists have confidence in the report? [1]

   ....

   (ii) Why would scientists look at the link between radon gas and lung cancer rather than other forms of cancer? [2]

   ....

   ....

   ....

P6 Radioactive Materials

(b) Explain why some scientists might question the correlation mentioned in the report. [6]

The quality of written communication will be assessed in your answer to this question.

....

....

....

....

....

....

....

5. Below are some statements about atoms. Put a tick (✓) in the box next to the correct statement. [1]

An atom consists of a nucleus containing protons with electrons in orbit around it. ☐

The nucleus of an atom contains protons and electrons. ☐

Neutrons are positively charged particles in the nucleus. ☐

There are only protons and neutrons in the nucleus of an atom. ☐

The nucleus of an atom is always radioactive. ☐

6. This question is about ionising radiation and its possible effects on the body.

   (a) Complete the following sentences. Use words from this list. You may use the words more than once.

   Alpha   Beta   Gamma

   (i) .... radiation causes harm if absorbed by cells but usually passes through the body without serious damage. [1]

   (ii) .... radiation is the most dangerous when the source is outside the body because it can penetrate the skin, causing internal damage. [1]

   (iii) .... radiation is the most dangerous if the source is inside the body as it is absorbed by cells in the body. [1]

   (iv) .... radiation is used to sterilise surgical instruments after they have been washed. [1]

Radioactive Materials — P6

(b) A teacher wants to demonstrate that certain materials can stop ionising radiation. He has three radioactive sources, each giving off a different ionising radiation. He also has a Geiger counter, a stopwatch, a piece of paper, a 4mm thick sheet of aluminium and a thick piece of lead.

(i) Explain how he could use the equipment safely to demonstrate the penetration properties of each ionising radiation.

The quality of written communication will be assessed in your answer to this question. [6]

(ii) Which ionising radiation has the greatest penetration? [1]

(iii) What other reading might the teacher take, using the stopwatch and Geiger counter, to make sure his results were accurate? [1]

(c) (i) Why would a teacher be worried about being exposed to ionising radiation from a source in a laboratory but would not be worried about being exposed to background radiation? [2]

(ii) What is the unit used to measure a dose of radiation? [1]

(iii) What does the word **irradiation** mean? [1]

P6 Radioactive Materials

7. This question is about the uses of radiation.

   (a) A patient is to have radioactive iodine injected into his body to treat a thyroid tumour. This will involve a doctor deciding what radioactive source to use, a radiologist preparing the radioactive iodine, a porter to take the patient to and from the radiology area in the hospital and a nurse to look after the patient whilst the activity of the radiation in the patient's body decreases to a safe level after a few days.

   (i) Which person will receive the highest lifetime dose of radiation? [1]

   (ii) Which person suffers contamination? [1]

   (iii) All five people will have been exposed to radiation. What word is used to describe this exposure to radiation? [1]

   (b) Another patient is in the hospital awaiting treatment for thyroid cancer. He is given a leaflet containing some information on the procedure. It says that radioiodine will be used, which emits beta particles and has a half-life of eight days.

   The patient is also given advice on what to do after the treatment:

   - You must remain in hospital for a few days.
   - You must be in a single room.
   - You must not get close to any visitors in hospital.

   The nurse advises the patient not to hug any relatives who come in to see him in the next few days. Why is that? [2]

8. This question is about whether a drug should be made available to treat a type of cancer. Read the article.

> Scientists carrying out research into a previously untreatable form of cancer have found some positive results from their tests.
>
> By adding a radioactive isotope to a certain antibody, scientists can target the tumours.
>
> Tumours are exposed to radiation for a few days but there is little damage to healthy cells. From a sample of 15 patients, 10 showed signs of responding either partially or fully to the drug.

   (a) What type of radiation is likely to be emitted from the radioactive source? [1]

Radioactive Materials P6

(b) Explain, giving your reasons, which source would be the most suitable to provide the radioactive isotope: a source with a half-life of a few hours, one with a half-life of a few days or one with a half-life of a few weeks.

The quality of written communication will be assessed in your answer to this question. [6]

9. This question is about radioactive sources and their properties.

The table gives information about four radioactive sources.

Source	Half-life	Radiation Emitted
W	1 hour	Alpha
X	40 years	Beta
Y	300 years	Alpha
Z	4 hours	Gamma

(a) Using the information in the table, choose the best source to match each of these uses.

(i) A source for a smoke detector which must have a short range and a small power of penetration. [1]

(ii) A source to act as a tracer with strong penetrating powers. [1]

(iii) A source to measure the thickness of thin aluminium cans on a conveyor belt. [1]

P6 Radioactive Materials

(b) Below are some statements about radioactive elements. Put ticks (✓) in the boxes next to the **three** correct statements. [3]

The time taken for a radioactive source to become safe is called the half-life. ☐

The half-life is a measurement of the background radiation. ☐

The activity of a radioactive source is constant. ☐

The time taken for the activity of a radioactive source to fall to half of its starting value is called the half-life. ☐

The term half-life can only be used with sources that emit gamma radiation. ☐

Most radioactive sources have the same half-life. ☐

The further you are from a radioactive source, the less radiation your body is exposed to. ☐

If you heat a radioactive source strongly, it will give off less radiation. ☐

Lead shields are used in hospitals to protect medical staff from exposure to radiation. ☐

Sources used inside the body have a long half-life. ☐

10. Complete the following sentences. Use words from this list. [3]

half-life   background count   alpha   beta   gamma

Chloe measured the time that the activity of a radioactive source took to fall from 60 decays per minute to 30 decays per minute. This time is called the _____ .

She found that the source emitted _____ radiation as the radiation was stopped by paper. She said that if she had used _____ radiation, she would have needed aluminium to stop it.

11. This question is about people who work with radioactive sources.

(a) (i) Why must exposure times be monitored for people who work with radioactive materials? [1]

....

....

(ii) Name one job in which a person is likely to come into contact with radiation. [1]

....

Radioactive Materials P6

(b) (i) Exposure to ionising radiation is known to be a cause of body cells developing cancer. Explain how ionising radiation can be used to treat and kill cancer cells. [2]

(ii) When treating cancer patients with ionising radiation, what are the dangers to the following people? [2]

The patient: ....

The medical staff: ....

(c) Give **two** precautions a person should take when working with radioactive sources. [2]

1. ....

2. ....

12. Below are some statements about radiation.

A Ionising radiation can be used as a tracer inside the body.

B Most radioactive waste from a power station is high-level waste.

C All elements emit ionising radiation.

D Low-level radioactive waste can be sealed and placed in landfill sites.

E Background radiation is the same throughout the UK.

Which of the statements are correct? Put a tick (✓) in the box next to the correct combination of statements. [1]

A and B ☐   A and D ☐   B, C and D ☐   A, C and E ☐
A, B and D ☐ B and E ☐   A, B and E ☐

13. Name **four** causes of background radiation. [4]

1. ....   2. ....
3. ....   4. ....

[Total: .... / 64]

P6 Radioactive Materials

Higher Tier

14. Below are nuclear equations for the decay of a uranium atom by emission of an alpha particle and for thorium as it decays by emitting a beta particle.

$$U^{238}_{92} \rightarrow Th^{v}_{90} + He^{4}_{w}$$

$$Th^{x}_{90} \rightarrow Pa^{234}_{91} + e^{0}_{y}$$

Four numbers have been replaced by letters. What numbers do v, w, x and y represent? [4]

v: .... w: ....

x: .... y: ....

15. This question is about radioactive decay.

(a) A group of students carried out an experiment to measure the half-life of protactinium using a stopwatch and a Geiger counter. Their results are shown in the table.

Time Measured (minutes)	0	1	2	3	4	5
Activity (counts per second)	251	127	63	31	30	7

(i) From the table, what is the best value for the half-life? Put a tick (✓) in the box next to the best answer. [1]

1 minute ☐

30 seconds ☐

2 minutes ☐

There is not enough information to calculate it. ☐

(ii) The students made a mistake recording their data. At what time did they record their outlier? Put a ring around the correct answer. [1]

1 minute   2 minutes   3 minutes   4 minutes   5 minutes

(b) One of the students weighed out 208g of a radioactive isotope which has a half-life of 3 days. How much of the isotope would be left after 15 days? [2]

.... g

(c) A radioactive isotope decays by emitting two alpha particles. Describe the changes in the nucleus of this isotope after emitting the two alpha particles. [2]

16. In a nuclear reactor, uranium is used to produce heat energy in the production of electricity. This question is about how the uranium fuel rods get hot and how the nuclear reactor is controlled.

(a) What happens when uranium undergoes nuclear fission?

The quality of written communication will be assessed in your answer to this question. [6]

(b) Nuclear fission can lead to a chain reaction. Briefly describe what happens in a chain reaction. [2]

(c) Explain how the chain reaction is controlled. [2]

P6 Radioactive Materials

17. Below are some statements about the differences between nuclei of the same element. Put ticks (✓) in the boxes next to the **two** correct statements. [2]

Isotopes of the same element always have the same number of protons. ☐

The number of neutrons in isotopes of the same element is always the same. ☐

All isotopes of an element are radioactive. ☐

Isotopes of an element always have the same half-life. ☐

Isotopes of an element always have the same number of protons but a different number of neutrons. ☐

Isotopes of an element always have the same number of neutrons but a different number of protons. ☐

18. This question is about radioactive decay.

(a) Explain one way in which ionising radiation emitted during the radioactive decay of a nucleus can be used as a tracer in the body. What safety procedures need to be considered? [4]

....

....

....

....

....

....

(b) If thorium (atomic number 90) was to emit one alpha particle and two beta particles, what nuclei would be produced? Put a tick (✓) in the box next to the correct answer. [1]

An isotope of thorium, atomic number 90 ☐

An isotope of uranium, atomic number 92 ☐

An isotope of protactinium, atomic number 91 ☐

Radioactive Materials — P6

19. This question is about the nucleus and the energy that can be liberated from it.

(a) The nucleus of an atom consists of protons and neutrons packed together. The protons carry a positive charge and neutrons have no charge. Explain why the nucleus does not disintegrate. [2]

(b) When a nucleus of uranium-235 fissions into barium-141 and krypton-92, the change in mass is 3.1×10^{-28} kg.

(i) Calculate the energy released by the fission of one uranium nucleus. [2]

.... J

(ii) Calculate how many nuclei must undergo fission in order to release 1.0J of energy by this reaction. [2]

[Total: .... / 33]

P7 Further Physics — Studying the Universe

1. **(a)** How long does it take the Sun to travel across the sky and appear in the same place the following day? Put a tick (✓) in the box next to the correct answer. [1]

   28 days ☐

   24 days ☐

   23 hours 56 minutes ☐

   24 hours ☐

   (b) In which direction does the Sun appear to travel across the sky? Put a tick (✓) in the box next to the correct answer. [1]

   North to south ☐

   East to west ☐

   South to north ☐

   West to east ☐

2. **(a)** Using the diagram to help you, explain why an observer on Earth is not able to see the same stars in January as in July. [2]

   ....

   ....

   ....

   (b) A star's declination is one measurement used to describe its position. Name another measurement that can be used. [1]

   ....

3. With the naked eye, the planets and stars look similar. How, therefore, can we tell the difference between the planets and stars? [2]

   ....

   ....

   ....

Further Physics — Studying the Universe P7

4. **(a)** How long does it take the Moon to travel east-west across the sky? Put a tick (✓) in the box next to the correct answer. [1]

Just under 24 hours ☐

Exactly 24 hours ☐

Just over 24 hours ☐

28 days ☐

(b) How long is the lunar cycle? Put a tick (✓) in the box next to the correct answer. [1]

1 day ☐

1 week ☐

28 days ☐

365 days ☐

(c) Complete the following sentences. Use words from this list. [4]

away from   **refracted**   **towards**   **reflected**
Sun   **Moon**   **light**

The Moon's appearance changes depending on which side of it we can see. Light from the Sun is

_____ from the _____. The side facing

_____ the Sun appears dark, whilst the side facing _____ the

Sun appears light.

(d) Explain why the Moon's appearance changes as it orbits the Earth. [2]

(e) If the Moon is directly over one point at midnight on one night, it will not be directly over the same point at midnight on the next night. Explain why this is so. [2]

P7 Further Physics — Studying the Universe

5. (a) During which phase of the Moon would a solar eclipse occur? Put a tick (✓) in the box next to the correct answer. [1]

New Moon ☐

Half Moon ☐

Crescent Moon ☐

Full Moon ☐

(b) The diagram shows a solar eclipse. Match the descriptions **A, B, C** and **D** with the labels 1–4 on the diagram. [3]

A Total eclipse ☐

B Partial eclipse ☐

C Earth ☐

D Moon ☐

6. (a) When light enters a lens, its path may change. What name is given to this change in direction and why does it occur? [2]

(b) What is another name for a convex lens? [1]

(c) In which direction are rays of light passing through a convex lens bent? [1]

(d) Complete the following sentences about convex lenses. Use words from this list. [3]

more   less   long   short

A weak lens has a .... curved surface and a .... focal length. A strong lens has a .... curved surface and a .... focal length.

Further Physics — Studying the Universe   P7

(e) (i) What unit is used to measure the power of a lens? [1]

(ii) A convex lens has a focal length of 50cm. What is the power of the lens? [2]

(f) The ray diagram below shows how a converging lens is used to produce an image of an object.

Describe the image formed in this diagram. [2]

7. (a) (i) What are the names of the two lenses used in a refracting telescope? [2]

1. ....

2. ....

(ii) Which of the lenses given in your answer to **(a)** part **(i)** is more curved? [1]

(b) How are reflecting telescopes different from refracting telescopes? Put a tick (✓) in the box next to the correct answer. [1]

They are cheaper. ☐   They use a mirror instead of a lens for the objective. ☐

They are smaller. ☐   They do not use an eyepiece. ☐

(c) Draw a diagram illustrating the path of light rays through a simple refracting telescope. Label the two different lenses. [3]

P7 Further Physics — Studying the Universe

8. (a) Some telescopes use a concave mirror instead of a convex lens. What is the advantage of using a mirror in terms of the images that can be seen? [2]

....

....

....

(b) On the diagram of the reflecting telescope, label the objective mirror and the eyepiece lens. [2]

9. (a) Light is a wave and its direction can be altered in **three** different ways. State these **three** ways. [3]

1. ....

2. ....

3. ....

(b) Water waves travel more slowly in shallow water than they do in deep water. Mark on the diagram how the waves would look in the example shown. [2]

Further Physics — Studying the Universe

(c) On the diagrams below, draw the path of a light ray as it enters and leaves the glass block. Label the normal and the angles of incidence and refraction. [2]

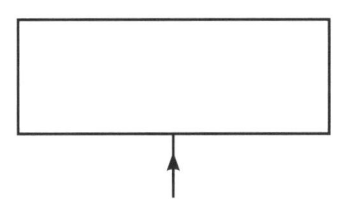

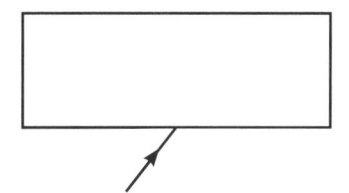

10. Explain why a light wave changes direction when it passes from air to glass and then from glass to air.

   ✏ *The quality of written communication will be assessed in your answer to this question.* [6]

   _____

   _____

   _____

   _____

   _____

   _____

   _____

11. (a) When waves pass through a narrow gap, they are diffracted. What does this mean? [1]

   _____

   (b) What happens when a wave passes through a gap much larger than its wavelength? [1]

   _____

   _____

P7 Further Physics — Studying the Universe

12. The diagram shows a house in the shadow of a hill. Use ideas about diffraction to explain why the house is able to receive the long-wave radio signals from the transmitter but microwave signals from the transmitter are unable to reach the house.

✏ *The quality of written communication will be assessed in your answer to this question.* [6]

13. (a) What is meant by the term **parallax angle**? [2]

(b) Read the statements about parallax. Put a tick (✓) in the correct box to show whether each statement is **true** or **false**. [3]

	true	false
(i) Parallax can only be used to measure the distance to planets.	☐	☐
(ii) An object that is further away from Earth will have a greater parallax angle than a closer object.	☐	☐
(iii) The observations used to find the parallax angle are made on opposite sides of the Earth.	☐	☐

Further Physics — Studying the Universe — P7

(c) On the diagram, draw and label the parallax angle. [1]

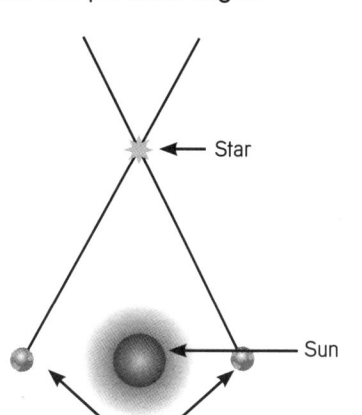

(d) Complete the table below. [4]

Star	Distance (pc)	Parallax Angle (arcseconds)
Sirius	2.64	
Arcturus		0.044
Barnard's Star		0.55
Proxima Centauri	1.30	

14. (a) A distant star has an observed parallax angle of 0.5 arcseconds. How far away is the star? [2]

....

.... parsecs

(b) Explain why it is only possible to measure the distance to relatively close stars and not to distant galaxies. [1]

....

....

(c) (i) What is a Cepheid variable star? [2]

....

....

P7 Further Physics — Studying the Universe

(ii) Describe how observations of Cepheid variable stars revealed the true nature of spiral nebulae.

✎ *The quality of written communication will be assessed in your answer to this question.* [6]

_____

_____

_____

_____

_____

_____

15. (a) What is meant by the **luminosity** of a star? [1]

_____

(b) What does the luminosity of a star depend on? Put ticks (✓) in the boxes next to the **two** correct answers. [2]

Its size ☐   Its temperature ☐   Its distance from Earth ☐   Its shape ☐

16. A galaxy is a distance of 80Mpc from Earth. If the Hubble constant is 70km/s per Mpc, calculate the speed of recession. [2]

_____

_____ km/s

17. This question is about gases and how the molecular model is used to explain their behaviour.

(a) (i) Explain, using a molecular model, how the pressure of a gas in a sealed cylinder changes at constant temperature if the volume is reduced by compressing the gas with a piston. [3]

_____

_____

_____

(ii) If the volume of the gas in the sealed cylinder had been kept constant and the temperature increased, explain in terms of the molecular model why the pressure would increase. [3]

_____

_____

_____

Further Physics — Studying the Universe P7

(b) (i) What is the value of absolute zero in Celsius? [1]

(ii) Explain, using a molecular model, what would happen to molecules at absolute zero. [4]

(c) The temperature of each of three gases was measured using two temperature sensors, one measuring in degrees Celsius and the other in Kelvin. Complete the table with the equivalent temperatures. [3]

Gas	Temperature (°C)	Temperature (K)
Oxygen	−20	
Helium		120
Water vapour	101	

(d) (i) A gas in a sealed container of constant volume is at a temperature of 20°C and has a pressure of 10^5 pascals. What would the pressure of the gas be if it was heated to 200°C? [2]

.... Pa

(ii) If the temperature of that gas in a sealed container had been constant at 20°C and the pressure had been doubled, what would have happened to the volume? [1]

18. This question is about star birth.

(a) Protostars form from clouds of gas which are compressed.

(i) What force causes the clouds of gas to compress? [1]

(ii) The cloud of gas must consist of mainly one element for a protostar to form. What is the element? [1]

P7 Further Physics — Studying the Universe

(iii) What will happen to the temperature of the gas as it is compressed? [1]

(b) Protostars become main sequence stars when a particular process begins.

(i) What is the name of this process? [1]

(ii) Complete the following sentence about the process in part (i). Use words from this list. [3]

    helium   hydrogen   atoms   energy

During this process four .... nuclei become one ....

nucleus with the release of ....

(c) An astronomer studies the spectrum from a protostar and also one from a star like the Sun.

(i) What difference will the astronomer notice between the spectrum from the protostar and that from the Sun? [1]

(ii) Explain why there is a difference. [2]

Further Physics — Studying the Universe P7

19. This question is about telescopes and the conditions under which they are used. Read the article.

| Greenwich is famous for its observatory which is situated close to the River Thames in south London. It is home to the 28-inch Grubb refracting telescope of 1893. | This is the largest of its kind in the UK. In 1947 the Royal Observatory moved the main telescopes from Greenwich to Herstmonceux Castle, which is in East Sussex. | The Isaac Newton Telescope was built by the observatory at Herstmonceux Castle in 1967 before being moved to Roque de los Muchachos in the Canary Islands in 1979. |

(a) The 28-inch Grubb refracting telescope is the largest of its kind in the UK. Why are there no very large refracting telescopes in use? [1]

(b) Suggest why in 1947 the Royal observatory moved to a less populated area. [1]

(c) Explain the advantages of moving the telescope from Herstmonceux Castle to the Canary Islands. [4]

(d) What difficulties might the observatory have experienced when the telescope was first set up in the Canary Islands in 1979? [3]

20. Astronomers working at an observatory can use different methods of operating telescopes to obtain useful data about different planets and galaxies. Describe **two** different ways in which a telescope could be used to record data from a planet. [2]

1.

2.

P7 Further Physics — Studying the Universe

21. Below are some statements about observatories. Put ticks (✓) in the boxes next to the **two** correct statements. [2]

The cost must be considered when building an observatory. ☐

Observatories are often built at altitude because few people live there. ☐

Telescopes with large mirrors are used to capture more light. ☐

The telescope will get better magnification at altitude than at sea level. ☐

22. This is the Hertzsprung–Russell diagram.

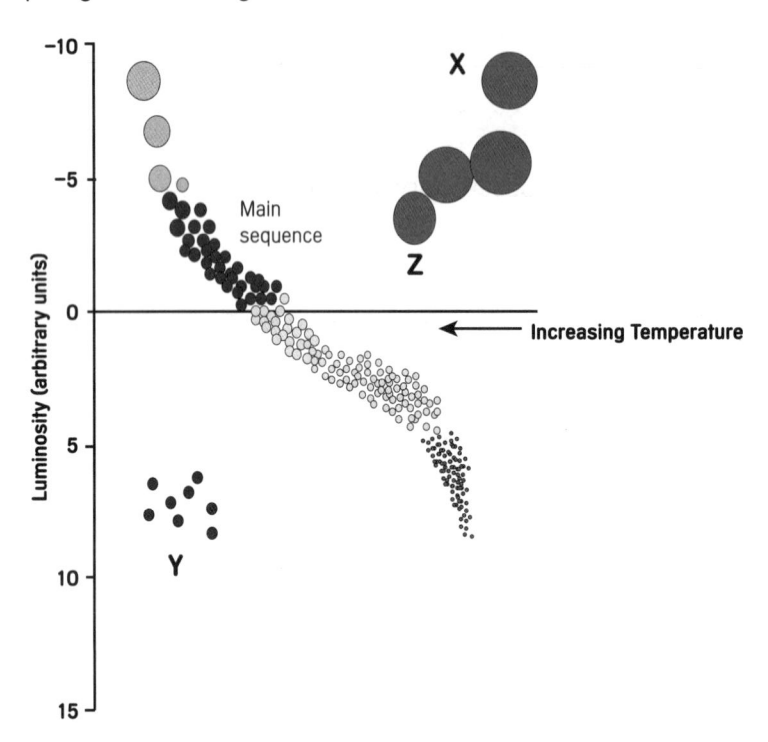

Which of the following statements are true? Put ticks (✓) in the boxes next to the **three** correct statements. [3]

Y is a white dwarf, Z is a supergiant and X is a red giant. ☐

Y is a cold star because it is dim. ☐

X is a supergiant, Y is a white dwarf and Z is a red giant. ☐

Z is a bright and hot star. ☐

The Sun would be approximately placed near the middle of the main sequence. ☐

The luminosity of a star decreases as it passes through the main sequence. ☐

A star in the middle of the main sequence is hotter than a white dwarf. ☐

Further Physics — Studying the Universe P7

23. There are several locations of major astronomical observatories. At each site it is necessary to consider the factors that make it a suitable place to build a large telescope. One such site is the Mauna Kea Observatories in Hawaii.

(a) Suggest **two** astronomical factors that made this an ideal site. [2]

1. ....

2. ....

(b) Give **two** examples of economic or other factors that might also be important when planning and building an observatory. [2]

1. ....

2. ....

(c) Telescopes such as the one built in Hawaii are reflectors. Suggest why a large refractor was not used instead. [2]

....

....

....

(d) The wavelength of light is very small, yet the telescope in Hawaii uses a large mirror to capture an image. Why is it an advantage to use a large mirror in the reflector? [2]

....

....

(e) A teacher explains that the telescopes in Chile are built well above sea level. A student then asks the teacher: "Why can't an observatory be built in Wales as it has mountains as well? Snowdon is 3560 feet above sea level."

Explain why this is not a good idea. [2]

....

....

....

© Lonsdale 83

P7 Further Physics — Studying the Universe

24. The diagram shows the relationship between luminosity and frequency for three stars. The vertical lines show the peak frequencies for each star.

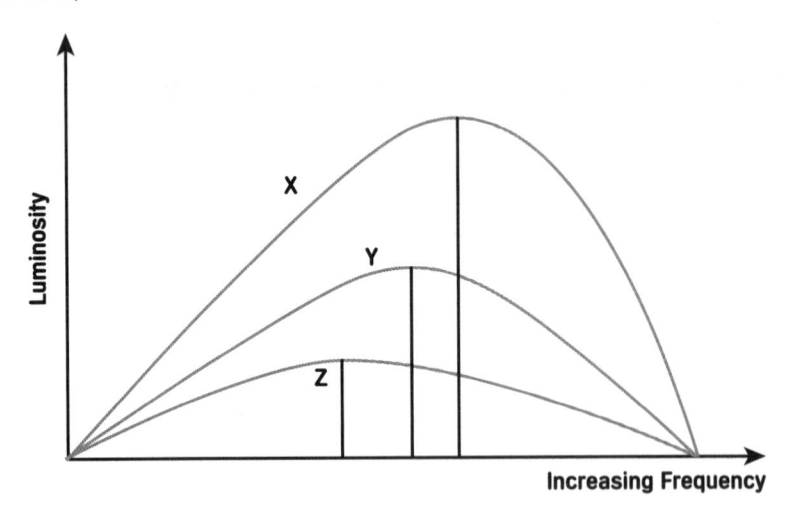

(a) A group of students is discussing the data shown in the graph.

Ben
Star Z is probably a red giant.

Alice
I think star Y is hotter than star Z.

Charlie
Star Y couldn't be a main sequence star.

Mel
Star X has the highest peak frequency so it must be hotter than star Y.

Which **two** students are making correct statements? [1]

_____ and _____

Further Physics — Studying the Universe P7

(b) Complete the following sentence. Use words from this list. [2]

density   **temperature**   **luminosity**   **rotation**

The peak frequency of star x is higher than that of star y. So for star x the _____

and the _____ must be higher than for star y.

25. This question is about nuclear fusion. The table gives the atomic masses of some elements.

Element	Hydrogen	Helium	Carbon	Nitrogen	Oxygen	Iron	Copper	Zinc
Atomic Mass (g)	1	4	12	14	16	56	64	65

(a) (i) Which **two** elements in the table are parts of the fusion process in main sequence stars such as the Sun? [2]

_____ and _____

(ii) Which **two** elements in the table are not products of nuclear fusion in the core of a star? [2]

_____ and _____

(b) Complete the following sentences. Use the names of elements in the table. [3]

In the core of a red giant, helium nuclei fuse to make _____ nuclei. There are

further reactions to produce heavier elements like _____

and _____ .

(c) How could elements heavier than iron have been formed? [1]

_____

(d) Why can further fusion reactions occur in the core of a red giant but not in the core of a main sequence star such as the Sun? [3]

_____

P7 Further Physics — Studying the Universe

26. The Sun is a main sequence star and Aldebaran is a red giant.

(a) (i) If an astronomer measured the temperature of the core of each of these stars, how would they compare? [1]

(ii) Explain why they would be different. [3]

(b) State how heat is transferred from the core of a star to the photosphere. [2]

27. This question is about the operation of telescopes and how they are used to explore the Universe.

(a) (i) Draw straight lines from the types of telescope to the main disadvantage of using them. [2]

Telescope	Main disadvantage
Hubble telescope	Images distorted by an unstable atmosphere
Jodrell Bank radio telescope	Affected most by diffraction
Newtonian reflector	Can be damaged by solar flares

(ii) Explain how the atmosphere can affect land-based telescopes.

✎ The quality of written communication will be assessed in your answer to this question. [6]

Further Physics — Studying the Universe P7

(b) The Hubble telescope was used to observe a star called Fomalhaut and it detected a very faint spot of light in 2004. The spot of light was, in fact, a planet. New observations in 2006 showed that the planet had moved and appeared to be in orbit around the star.

(i) What name do astronomers give to planets belonging to stars other than our Sun? [1]

(ii) What other observations, apart from seeing a faint light, might lead astronomers to think that a distant star has a planetary system around it? [2]

(iii) What advantage did the Hubble telescope have over land-based telescopes that allowed it to detect such a dim and distant object? [2]

(iv) Two students are discussing the merit of spending money on the Hubble telescope.

Tosin
I would much rather the money be spent on useful things like better hospitals and schools.

Gemma
If we don't understand what is around us, how can we plan for a better future? We need to understand how the solar system formed.

How can the discoveries of planets around other stars like Fomalhaut help support Gemma's comment to Tosin? [2]

P7 Further Physics — Studying the Universe

28. This question is about the emission of energy by stars.

(a) The table shows the temperature of five stars.

Star	Sun	Antares	Spica	Vega	Canopus
Temperature (K)	5800	3400	23 000	9300	7300

(i) What is the temperature of the star Antares in degrees Celsius? [1]

....

(ii) Which star would have both the highest luminosity and the highest peak frequency?
Put a (ring) around the correct answer. [1]

       Sun   Antares   Spica   Vega   Canopus

(iii) Which star is most likely to be a red giant? Put a (ring) around the correct answer. [1]

       Sun   Antares   Spica   Vega   Canopus

(b) Sometimes telescopes detect a sudden increase in the energy released from a supergiant star. This is due to a supernova.

(i) Describe the composition of the core of a supergiant just before it becomes a supernova. [1]

....

(ii) What types of nuclei are generated when a star explodes as a supernova? [1]

....

29. Below are some statements about stars and their life cycle.

A The Sun could not become a black hole when fusion stops.

B A red giant appears red because it is very hot.

C In a white dwarf star there is no nuclear fusion.

D A low mass star can compress the core further at the end of helium fusion.

E The photosphere of a star cools if it expands at the end of the main sequence to form a red giant.

Which statements are correct? Put a tick (✓) in the box next to the correct combination of statements. [1]

A, C and E ☐   B, D and E ☐   B, C and D ☐

A, D and E ☐   A, C, D and E ☐   All of them ☐

Further Physics — Studying the Universe | P7

30. This question is about how telescopes are used to view the Universe.

(a) The Search for Extraterrestrial Intelligence (SETI) project has involved the use of radio telescopes since 1994 to listen for any signals reaching the Earth that could come from an intelligent life form.

   (i) Why is it so difficult to be sure that any signals reaching the Earth will be detected? [2]

   (ii) So far no signals have been detected. Why would it be wrong to conclude that this means no intelligent life exists elsewhere in the Universe? [2]

(b) The Arecibo radio telescope in Puerto Rico has been used to collect data for use by astronomers supporting the SETI project. Why can this telescope be based on the Earth's surface whilst the Hubble telescope is orbiting above the Earth's atmosphere? [2]

(c) A radio dish has to be very large to receive radio waves. Explain why radio signals do not generally give as sharp an image as an optical telescope with a large mirror. [2]

P7 Further Physics — Studying the Universe

31. This question is about the construction of observatories and the maintenance of telescopes in space.

(a) The Hubble telescope has been very successful but has also experienced some operational problems that have been difficult to solve.

Explain **two** advantages and **two** disadvantages of operating a telescope like Hubble which is orbiting outside the Earth's atmosphere.

The quality of written communication will be assessed in your answer to this question. [6]

(b) The Gemini Observatory in Chile was a result of shared work between Australia and six other countries.

(i) Describe **two** benefits of sharing the work of setting up an observatory, rather than just one country being responsible. [2]

1. ....

2. ....

(ii) Astronomers from the countries which worked together in constructing the telescope will expect to access it. State **three** ways in which astronomers could control the telescope. [3]

1. ....

2. ....

3. ....

(c) When planning, building, operating or closing down an observatory, what non-astronomical factors need to be considered? [3]

Further Physics — Studying the Universe   P7

(d) Stars emit radiation from several regions of the electromagnetic spectrum. Astronomers need to study radiation from these different regions of the electromagnetic spectrum.

  (i) Give examples of **three** different types of telescope used by astronomers. [3]

   1. _____

   2. _____

   3. _____

  (ii) Explain why some types of telescope have to be operated above the Earth's atmosphere in space. [2]

   _____

   _____

   _____

   _____

32. Read the article.

| Astronomers study spectra from distant stars. Each element produces a different collection of coloured lines, which can be used to identify the elements that are present in the star. | Information is then gained about the type of star being observed, including its age and the chance of planets orbiting that star. | This data is recorded and shared with other astronomers before a map can be produced and published of the night sky. |

(a) What types of star might be included on the map? Give **three** examples. [2]

_____

_____

(b) Explain how spectra from a star can be used to help identify the type or composition of the star.

✏ *The quality of written communication will be assessed in your answer to this question.* [6]

_____

_____

_____

_____

_____

P7 Further Physics — Studying the Universe

(c) Explain why astronomers might share their information before publishing a map of the night sky. [1]

....

....

33. Many exoplanets have been discovered since the first one in 1992. Most have been giant planets of a size similar to Jupiter.

(a) Where does the light come from that could make an exoplanet visible? Put a ring around the correct answer. [1]

        The Sun   **A supernova**   **Nuclear fusion**

           A close star   **A galaxy**

(b) Give **two** ways in which exoplanets that cannot be seen directly can be detected. [2]

1. ....

....

2. ....

....

(c) Why would direct observation of exoplanets only be possible using very large diameter telescopes? [1]

....

....

34. Computers play an important part in modern astronomy.

Give **three** advantages of using computer-controlled telescopes. [3]

1. ....

....

2. ....

....

3. ....

....

Further Physics — Studying the Universe P7

35. (a) (i) At what stage in a star's life cycle does a supernova occur? [1]

(ii) Briefly describe what happens when a supernova occurs. [1]

(iii) What may remain after a supernova has occurred? [2]

(b) (i) What will happen to our Sun after it leaves the main sequence? [2]

(ii) The Sun will eventually become a planetary nebula. The outer layers will move off into space leaving the core behind. Which of the four answers best describes the core of the Sun? Put a tick (✓) in the box next to the correct answer. [1]

A black hole ☐

A white dwarf ☐

A red dwarf ☐

A neutron star ☐

(c) State a factor that determines the eventual fate of a star. [1]

[Total: .... / 236]

Higher Tier

36. Complete the following sentences. Use words from this list. [3]

equator   horizon   negative   positive   zero

Stars with a _____ declination are visible from the northern hemisphere.

Stars with a _____ declination are visible from the southern hemisphere.

If a star has a zero declination, it can be seen above the _____ .

P7 Further Physics — Studying the Universe

37. Four young astronomers were discussing some observations that they had been making using a large reflecting telescope.

Ciara
I was observing a star as its luminosity changed.

Evelyn
I have been studying a Cepheid variable for several weeks.

Bryson
It is wonderful to be able to see so many stars in a distant galaxy.

Cindy
I am able to add false colour to my images.

(a) (i) Which two astronomers are talking of the advantages of using computer-controlled telescopes? [1]

_____ and _____

(ii) Who might be talking about exoplanets? [1]

_____

(b) Evelyn has been studying a Cepheid variable for several weeks.

(i) What **two** measurements will she be recording? [2]

_____

(ii) What conclusion can she make from her measurements? [1]

_____

Further Physics — Studying the Universe P7

(c) Other astronomers are repeating Evelyn's measurements for other Cepheid variables in other galaxies. Explain how their work and measurements of red shift from those galaxies can be used to find a value for the Hubble constant. [3]

38. (a) In 1920, a famous debate about the scale of the Universe took place. Give the names of the **two** main astronomers involved in the debate. [2]

.... and ....

(b) What was the name originally given to the 'fuzzy objects' observed in the night sky that played a major role in this debate? [1]

(c) Outline the opinions held by the two opposing astronomers about what these fuzzy objects were and the evidence they used to support them.

✎ *The quality of written communication will be assessed in your answer to this question.* [6]

(d) In the mid-1920s, Edwin Hubble discovered that the fuzzy objects were further away than any star in the Milky Way galaxy. What did Hubble observe to draw him to this conclusion? [1]

P7 Further Physics — Studying the Universe

(e) What did Edwin Hubble discover about the Universe? Put a tick (✓) in the box next to the correct answer. [1]

It is expanding. ☐

It is shrinking. ☐

It is staying the same size. ☐

It started with a 'Big Bang'. ☐

39. This question is about stars.

(a) A student is using a balloon to investigate how the change in volume of a gas in a star might affect the pressure. If the temperature of the spherical balloon is kept constant, by what factor will the pressure change if the radius of the balloon is doubled? [3]

....

....

....

(b) Below are some equations for fusion reactions.

$x\,{}^{4}_{2}He \longrightarrow {}^{12}_{6}C$

${}^{1}_{1}H + {}^{12}_{6}C \longrightarrow {}^{y}_{7}N$

${}^{4}_{2}He + {}^{12}_{z}C \longrightarrow {}^{16}_{8}O$

What are the values of x, y and z? [3]

x = ...

y = ...

z = ...

(c) Stars produce absorption spectra which can be used to identify the elements present in that star. Explain how electron energy levels within atoms give rise to absorption spectra. [3]

....

....

....

....

[Total: .... / 31]

Data Sheet

Useful Relationships

The Earth in the Universe

Distance = Wave speed × Time

Wave speed = Frequency × Wavelength

Sustainable Energy

Energy transferred = Power × Time

Power = Voltage × Current

Efficiency = $\dfrac{\text{Energy usefully transferred}}{\text{Total energy supplied}}$ × 100%

Explaining Motion

Speed = $\dfrac{\text{Distance travelled}}{\text{Time taken}}$

Acceleration = $\dfrac{\text{Change in velocity}}{\text{Time taken}}$

Momentum = Mass × Velocity

Change of momentum = Resultant force × Time for which it acts

Work done by a force = Force × Distance moved in the direction of the force

Amount of energy transferred = Work done

Change in gravitational potential energy = Weight × Vertical height difference

Kinetic energy = $\dfrac{1}{2}$ × Mass × [Velocity]^2

Data Sheet

Electric Circuits

Power = Voltage × Current

Resistance = $\dfrac{\text{Voltage}}{\text{Current}}$

$\dfrac{\text{Voltage across primary coil}}{\text{Voltage across secondary coil}} = \dfrac{\text{Number of turns in primary coil}}{\text{Number of turns in secondary coil}}$

Radioactive Materials

Energy = Mass × [Speed of light in a vacuum]^2

Observing the Universe

Lens power = $\dfrac{1}{\text{Focal length}}$

Magnification = $\dfrac{\text{Focal length of objective lens}}{\text{Focal length of eyepiece lens}}$

Speed of recession = Hubble constant × Distance

Pressure × Volume = Constant

$\dfrac{\text{Pressure}}{\text{Temperature}}$ = Constant

$\dfrac{\text{Volume}}{\text{Temperature}}$ = Constant

Energy = Mass × [Speed of light in a vacuum]^2

Notes

Notes